P9-CDD-489

Twayne's United States Authors Series

EDITOR OF THIS VOLUME

Mason I. Lowance, Jr.

University of Massachusetts, Amherst

Royall Tyler

TUSAS 344

Royall Tyler

ROYALL TYLER

By ADA LOU CARSON
and
HERBERT L. CARSON

Ferris State College

TWAYNE PUBLISHERS
A DIVISION OF G. K. HALL & CO., BOSTON

Published in 1979 by Twayne Publishers,
A Division of G. K. Hall & Co.

Printed on permanent/durable acid-free paper and bound
in the United States of America

First Printing

Library of Congress Cataloging in Publication Data

Carson, Ada Lou.
Royall Tyler.

(Twayne's United States authors series ; TUSAS 344)
Bibliography: p. 152-61
Includes index.
1. Tyler, Royall, 1757-1826—Criticism and interpretation.
I. Carson, Herbert L., joint author.
PS855.T7Z6 818'.2'09 79-4621
ISBN 0-8057-7281-2

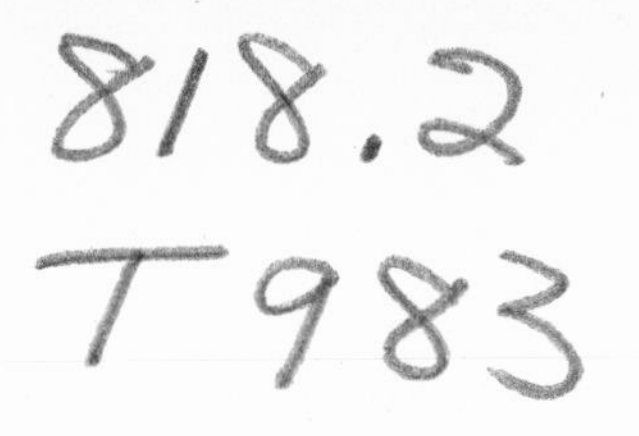

In Honor
of Our Parents
and Our Children

Contents

About the Authors

Ada Lou Carson received her B.A. from the University of Pittsburgh (*magna cum laude*, Phi Beta Kappa). She received her M.A. from Columbia University and is a doctoral candidate at the University of Minnesota. Mrs. Carson has taught in public schools as well as at the University of Minnesota. Presently she is an Assistant Professor of English at Ferris State College in Michigan. Listed in *Michigan Authors,* Mrs. Carson has published widely, including articles for *College Composition and Communication*, book reviews for the Grand Rapids *Press,* and special syllabi on American literature for the University of Minnesota. Her anthology *The Impact of Fiction* has been used by colleges in this country and Canada.

Herbert L. Carson received his B.A. from the University of Pittsburgh, his M.A. from Columbia University, and his Ph.D. from the University of Minnesota. He has taught at the University of Minnesota, the University of Nebraska, and Youngstown University. He is presently Professor of Humanities and Literature at Ferris State College. Dr. Carson is also a member of the Board of the Michigan Council for the Humanities, a state-based agency of the National Endowment for the Humanities. He has published articles, fiction, and poetry in numerous periodicals, as well as frequently reviewing books for the Grand Rapids *Press*. He published a textbook *Steps in Successful Speaking* and, with Mrs. Carson, he edited *The Impact of Fiction*.

Preface

Royall Tyler (1757 - 1826) was the author of *The Contrast*, the first American comic drama to be professionally produced in the United States. If Tyler is known at all to students of American literature, it is for this play. Tyler, however, deserves more attention than has yet been accorded to him. The purpose of our book is to stimulate interest in and appreciation for the work of Royall Tyler.

Tyler is of greater historical significance than is usually realized. Besides America's first comic drama, he also wrote its first musical play. He wrote one of the first novels about life in New England and was one of the nation's earliest local colorists. He was one of the first Americans to use fiction as a weapon against slavery. He was an early commentator on the dynamics of language. He was one of America's first periodical columnists. He helped correct American manners and literary tastes by satirizing the foibles of his countrymen. He frequently expressed the need for the United States to develop a native literature and to refine its own customs and manners rather than imitating European ways. Our book provides information about Tyler's many literary achievements.

Tyler's writing career is an example of the predicament of a man of literature during this nation's formative years, when people believed that "it is impossible to be at once a man of business and a man of rhyme. . . ."[1] In addition, Tyler's works can virtually serve as an index to the attitudes, the reading habits, and the general interests of educated Americans in the late eighteenth and early nineteenth centuries. For these reasons, as well as for his moments of literary skill, Royall Tyler should be better known to readers of American literature.

One reason for the neglect of Tyler is the fact that his papers, which are stored at the Vermont Historical Society, were not made available to scholars until 1964.[2] Since that time, a critical biography of Tyler and several editions of his works have appeared.

Our book begins with a survey of Tyler's life and works. We discuss his family, his youth and education, his busy career as a frontier jurist, and such personal stories as his unsuccessful courtship of

John Adams's daughter Nabby. Later chapters explain how these activities are reflected in Tyler's writings.

Our book is a study of Tyler's writings. Chapter 2 deals with *The Contrast* (1787). An analytical summary of the play is given, followed by our critical comments. This chapter explains how *The Contrast* came to be written, its stage history, the authorship of the songs, and the responses of various critics from 1787 to modern times. Sources that may have influenced the writing of the play are discussed, as well as the play's significance and influence. Tyler's creation of the Yankee, an important stage type, is given detailed coverage. Chapter 2 contains a full range of information and comments about *The Contrast*.

Chapter 3 deals with Tyler's other plays, none of which is of the same quality as his first. As much information as possible is provided about Tyler's lost plays. Fortunately, the lyrics of the songs in his second play, *May Day in Town* (1787), were recently discovered.[3] These lyrics suggest the plot of the missing musical play and are discussed here for the first time in a full-length work. Chapter 3 also covers Tyler's extant plays in detail, providing analytical summaries, stage history, critical responses, and general information about *The Island of Barrataria* (probably written after 1813) and the three biblical dramas—*Joseph and His Brethren, The Judgement of Solomon,* and *The Origin of the Feast of Purim* (all written *c.* 1824 - 25). Some new information about the date of composition of *The Island of Barrataria* is made available here for the first time.

Tyler's comic adventure novel, *The Algerine Captive* (1797), is the main subject of Chapter 4. *Captive* was one of the first American novels to describe life in pre-Revolutionary New England. It was one of the first American novels to be reprinted in England. *Captive* is an early example of antislavery fiction. Tyler frequently inveighed against slavery as both a judge and a writer.

In his last years, Tyler attempted to revise Volume I of *The Algerine Captive*. This uncompleted revision, *The Bay Boy* (*c.* 1824), is discussed in analytical detail in the last section of Chapter 4. *The Bay Boy* is a fine example of local-color writing. It provides valuable information about the life and customs of pre-Revolutionary New England. *The Bay Boy* is also delightful reading and may well be Tyler's masterpiece.

A "minor classic"[4] by Tyler is his series of fictional letters from an American abroad, *The Yankey in London* (1809). Chapter 5 provides a critical analysis of these letters and summaries of the

Yankey's more incisive comments about government, law, literature, and the foibles of humanity. The Yankey's surprisingly modern theories about the dynamics of language are also discussed. *Yankey*'s publishing history and the responses of critics are given. Like many of Tyler's works, *Yankey* is a good source of information about literary tastes at the turn of the nineteenth century.

Chapter 6 treats Tyler's miscellaneous prose; Chapter 7, his poetry. Most of Tyler's essays and verse first appeared in journals and newspapers. Often these contributions were not signed with his name. We explain how attributions are made. For our discussion of Tyler's prose and poetry, we have used the most easily available sources, so that interested readers may consult the complete selections without difficulty. The discussion of Tyler's prose and poetry includes the history of Tyler's collaboration with one of America's first professional men of letters, Joseph Dennie. In 1794 Tyler and Dennie began one of America's earliest newspaper columns, Colon & Spondee.

Because Tyler's fugitive essays and poems are so numerous, limitations of space have prevented us from discussing all of them. In Chapters 6 and 7, we refer at least briefly to the most interesting, the best written, the most significant, and the most representative of Tyler's essays and poems. We include comments by critics, explain any problems of attribution and dating, and explore the sources of Tyler's materials.

Chapter 6 covers all of Tyler's extant sermons, speeches, and law reports, including his two-volume *Reports of Cases. . . .* The chapter also discusses a large number of Tyler's essays. These essays frequently provide a humorous commentary on life in the new nation. Among other topics, the essays deal with heroes like George Washington and villains (to Tyler) like Tom Paine, and with Indians, patriotism, government, literature, and marriage.

Tyler's poetry is the subject of Chapter 7. The verse provides a rich mine of information about American life. Tyler's humorous poems, especially his satires, are among his best works. A more serious poem, "The Chestnut Tree" (*c.* 1824), includes early comments about the problems of industrialization in the United States. Tyler's poems are often didactic. In them, the author expresses his ideas about women and marriage, fashions, drinking, literature and the theater, patriotism, slavery, politics, and various melancholy subjects such as old age, sickness, and death.

Tyler was an able writer of humor and local color. His work

provides valuable descriptions of the life, customs, reading tastes, and general attitudes of the times. For his literary achievements, his pioneering efforts as an American writer, and the insights he provides into our origins as a people, Tyler is an important figure.

In addition, despite his haste and unwillingness to revise, Tyler was a skillful writer. He produced some specific works which deserve respect as literary accomplishments: *The Contrast,* "The Origin of Evil," Volume I of *The Algerine Captive* and its brilliant reworking as *The Bay Boy, The Yankey in London,* the Colon & Spondee satires, the Della Cruscan satires, *The Island of Barrataria,* and "The Chestnut Tree." These and many other works are analyzed in our book. By providing fresh perspectives on these works, we hope to stimulate new interest in and appreciation for the writing of Royall Tyler.

Tyler and many of his friends and family were casual spellers. To avoid the continual use of "*sic*" we have copied exactly the spelling of the source listed in the Notes and References section.

This book could not have been completed without the encouragement and cooperation of a number of people and institutions. A summer grant from Ferris State College gave Dr. Carson time to work on the book. Dr. Harold Wisner, Chairman of the Humanities Department, and his secretary, Mrs. Bernadine Vaughn, have been extremely cooperative and helpful. Many of our colleagues at Ferris State College aided us with our work, including Dr. John Johnson and Dr. Cornelius Eringaard.

We would also like to express our thanks to Mrs. Laura Abbott and Mrs. Reidun Nuquist at the Vermont Historical Society, to Mr. John L. Buechler and the staff at the University of Vermont Library, to Royall Tyler's descendant Mrs. Dorothy Sutherland Melville, who provided us with a copy of Royall Tyler, Jr.'s *The Speculators,* to Professor Edward M. Griffin at the University of Minnesota, and to the Ferris State College library—especially to Mrs. Mary Braun, who arranged innumerable interlibrary loans for us, and to Mr. R. Lawrence Martin. Our thanks go to the many Tyler scholars who have corresponded with us. We also appreciate the assistance and forebearance of our children—Bill, Winky, and Bryan.

While we appreciate the help of all these people, we of course take full responsibility for the contents of this book. Royall Tyler and his family are congenial subjects for study; we hope that this congeniality can be shared with our readers.

Chronology

1757 William Clark Tyler born July 18 in Boston, Massachusetts.

1771 After his father's death, William Clark Tyler changed his name to Royall Tyler.

1772 Entered Harvard University.

1776 B.A. from Harvard; honorary B.A. from Yale; joined Boston Independent Co. under John Hancock.

1778 Commissioned as Brigade Major of the Light Corps under General John Sullivan; served at Battle of Newport, Rhode Island.

1779 M.A. from Harvard for studies in law.

1780 Admitted to the bar of Massachusetts.

1782 Practiced law in Braintree (now Quincy), Massachusetts. Met Abigail Adams, daughter of John Adams.

1785 Engagement to Abigail Adams ended.

1787 Aide to General Benjamin Lincoln during Shays' Rebellion. In March, sent to New York. On April 16, the American Company staged *The Contrast*, the first American comedy to be professionally produced. On May 19, the American Company staged *May Day in Town*, a comic opera.

1790 *The Contrast* published. Tyler moved to Vermont.

1793 "The Origin of Evil, An Elegy," published.

1794 Became State's Attorney for Windham County, Vermont. Married Mary Palmer. Began Colon & Spondee series with Joseph Dennie.

1797 *The Algerine Captive* published. *The Georgia Spec*, a play, produced in Boston.

1801 Elected Assistant Judge of the Vermont Supreme Court.

1807 Elected Chief Justice of the Vermont Supreme Court.

1808 *The Trial of Cyrus B. Dean* published.

1809 *The Yankey in London* and *Reports of Cases Argued . . . in the Supreme Court . . . of Vermont* (Volume I), published by Isaac Riley. Volume II of *Reports* published in 1810.

1811 Appointed Professor of Jurisprudence, University of Vermont; services ended in 1814.

1812 Failed to win election to United States Senate.
1813 Not reelected to Vermont Supreme Court.
1815 Appointed Register of Probate, Windham County, Vermont.
1822 Not reappointed as Register of Probate. His health failing, Tyler was hereafter supported financially by family, friends, and neighbors.
1824 Worked on three sacred dramas, plus *The Bay Boy*, "The
1825 Chestnut Tree," and portions of "Utile Dulci."
1826 Died on August 16, 1826.
1866 Mary Palmer Tyler died, July 7.
1931 "The Chestnut Tree," a poem (*c.* 1824) first published.
1941 Four plays published: *The Island of Barrataria* and three sacred dramas—*Joseph and His Brethren, The Judgement of Solomon,* and *The Origin of the Feast of Purim.*
1967 *Royall Tyler,* by G. Thomas Tanselle, published; first comprehensive study of Tyler. Facsimile of *The Algerine Captive* published, introduction by Jack B. Moore.
1968 *The Verse of Royall Tyler* published, edited by Marius B. Péladeau.
1970 Modern edition of *The Algerine Captive* published, edited by Don L. Cook.
1972 *The Prose of Royall Tyler* published, edited by Marius B. Péladeau.
1974 Royall Tyler Theatre dedicated at University of Vermont. Broadside containing words to songs from *May Day in Town* discovered at Harvard Library by Katherine S. Jarvis.
1978 Modern edition of *The Bay Boy* published, edited by Martha R. Wright.

CHAPTER 1

A New England Wit and Patriot

THOSE were times that tried men's souls. The American colonists were becoming increasingly angered with the mother country. Revolution was in the air, and nowhere more than in Boston. On Ann Street, just north of Faneuil Hall, the Tyler family lived.[1] Boston must have been an exciting place for young William Clark Tyler, later to take his father's name of Royall Tyler. William Clark Tyler ". . . was growing to Boyhood. The fireworks[,] processions, pealing of bells, and salvos of artillery, which marked the brief intoxication of loyalty on the repeal of the Stamp Act, was to him a childish, though vivid memory. . . ."[2]

I *The Tylers of Boston (1680 - 1771)*

William Clark Tyler was a descendant of Thomas Tyler, an Englishman from Devonshire. Thomas, the captain of a merchant ship, had settled in Boston around 1680 and was lost at sea in 1703.[3] Thomas's son, William (1688 - 1755), entered trade in Boston. William was an active citizen and deacon of his church. He also occupied the office of Overseer of the Poor.[4] William married Sarah Royall (1688 - 1740). One of their sons was the first Royall Tyler, father of the playwright. This first Royall Tyler was born on September 8, 1724. After his graduation from Harvard in 1743, he joined his father, importing and retailing English manufactured goods.[5] In 1747, Royall Tyler married Mary Steele, the daughter of Captain John Steele.[6]

The first Royall Tyler quickly became active in public affairs. Records indicate that he assumed many duties, including that of School Visitor and Overseer of the Poor.[7] In 1758, Tyler was elected to the office of Justice of the Peace. The following year, he filled a vacant seat in the Massachusetts House of Representatives, remaining a member of the House until 1764. Tyler was a member of the Sons of Liberty.[8] He led the committee which objected to the

British tax on colonial shipping. He was chairman of the committee appointed after the Boston Massacre to protest the quartering of British troops in Boston.[9] Tyler was also on the King's Council from 1764 until his death on May 20, 1771.[10]

Tyler's marriage to Mary Steele resulted in four children—two girls, Mary and Jane; and two boys, John Steele and William Clark.[11] According to family tradition, Royall Tyler's will disinherited his older son, John Steele. The estate went wholly to Tyler's younger son, William Clark, who had been born on July 18, 1757. After his father's death, William Clark Tyler acceded to his mother's request and legally changed his name to Royall Tyler.[12] This Royall Tyler was to become the author of *The Contrast*.

The young Royall Tyler entered Harvard College on July 15, 1772.[13] In October of that year, Tyler's mother remarried and moved to Jamaica Plain, Massachusetts. Her second husband was William Whitwell, a Boston merchant.[14] For Royall Tyler and for the colonies, an important era was beginning.

II *The Harvard Years (1771 - 1776)*

At Harvard, the students were deeply involved with the events of the time.[15] Royall Tyler's classmates at college included future judges, congressmen, senators, and governors.[16] Studying Latin and Greek and discussing political interests did not occupy all of the students' time. Tyler's son and biographer noted that his father was apparently involved in some "serious escapades. . . ."[17] The biographer gives no details about these reports, commenting that they were "doubtless. . .exaggerations. . . ."[18]

In July 1776, shortly after the Declaration of Independence was signed, Royall Tyler was granted his Bachelor of Arts degree by Harvard.[19] In October of the same year, Yale University granted Tyler an honorary Bachelor of Arts degree. Whether this was "a singular honor" or a "collegiate courtesy" is uncertain.[20]

III *Years of War and Law (1776 - 1780)*

Tyler joined the Revolutionary Army in December 1776: "Tyler, Royall. List of men subscribing to regulations for formation of an Independent co. to be raised in Boston; officers of said Boston Independent co. . . . Major Gen John Hancock to serve as Lieutenant Colonel."[21] However, Tyler did not see much military service with the Independent Company because his mother was reluctant to have him participate in military action. Her second husband had died in 1775, and her older son, John Steele Tyler, had been sent by General Washington on a number of spy missions.[22]

Despite Royall Tyler's enlistment, after his graduation he read law in Cambridge and Boston, studying with Francis Dana and Benjamin Hichborn.[23] Apparently, Tyler did not devote himself exclusively to these studies. With two friends, Tyler was accused in 1777 of profanity, noises, and breaking windows in Cambridge.[24] Years later Tyler, briefly contemplating becoming a minister, looked back with regret on some of his earlier escapades.[25]

Tyler was one of a group of "remarkably brilliant" young men who met in the rooms of the painter John Trumbull.[26] In 1778 several of these young men joined the military service as aides to General John Sullivan. Tyler was commissioned Brigade Major of the Light Corps, and apparently was present in August 1778 at the unsuccessful attempt by General Sullivan to take Newport, Rhode Island, from the British.[27]

This service seems to have been Tyler's only active duty during the Revolutionary War. His military participation did not interfere with his studies of law. He received a Master of Arts degree from Harvard University in 1779.[28] That year, Tyler moved briefly to Falmouth (now Portland), Maine.[29] On August 19, 1780, Tyler was admitted to the bar of Massachusetts.[30] In the fall of 1782, Tyler settled at Braintree (now Quincy), Massachusetts. Here Royall Tyler was to come within the orbit of a future President of the United States.

IV *An American Romance (1780 - 1786)*

Braintree was a village some eight miles from Boston. In the small community, a lawyer of Tyler's wit and talent soon became prominent.[31] He roomed with the family of Richard Cranch, whose wife was the sister of Mrs. John Adams.[32] The Cranch family was also related to the family of Joseph Pearse Palmer, a prominent merchant. The Adamses, Cranches, and Palmers were at the top of the social scale in Braintree. Tyler moved easily within this group. Here he met young Abigail Adams, daughter of John and Abigail. The seventeen-year-old Abigail, nicknamed "Nabby," was a clever and beautiful girl.

At first Nabby was suspicious that Tyler was "practicing upon Chesterfields plan, that is the essence & quintessence of artfulness. . . ."[33] The head of the family, John Adams, was in Europe negotiating the peace treaty between the United States and Great Britain. On December 23, 1782, Mrs. Adams wrote about Tyler to her husband: "[W]e have in the little circle an other Gentleman who has opend an office in Town. . . . having a very pretty patrimony left him, possessing a sprightly fancy, a warm imagination and an agreable person, he was rather negligent in persueing his buisness . . . and dissipated two or 3 years of his Life and too much of his fortune for to reflect upon with pleasure. . . . I am not acquainted with any young Gentleman whose attainments in literature are equal to his, who judges with greater accuracy or discovers a more delicate and refined taste."[34] In the same letter, Mrs. Adams mentions a growing attachment between young Nabby and Tyler.

John Adams's initial response (January 22, 1783) was unfriendly: "I confess I dont like the Subject at all. . . . My Child is a Model . . . and is not to be the Prize, I hope of any, even reformed Rake."[35] For a son-in-law Adams did not want "a poet nor a professor of the belle letters." He continued, "I positively forbid any connection between my daughter and any youth upon earth who does not totally eradicate every taste for gaiety and expense."[36] Apparently Mrs. Adams managed to break off the romance for a time. Nabby went to Boston during the remainder of the winter of 1783. The young people now considered themselves merely friends.[37]

Tyler looked after his law business and purchased a farm near Braintree.[38] Assisted by his status as a landowner, Tyler began to ingratiate himself with Mrs. Adams. She reported to her husband (December 27, 1783), ". . . I believe this Gentleman has . . . a hope that he may not be considered unworthy a connection in this family."[39] Tyler assisted Mrs. Adams with her husband's accounts and collected some money owed to Adams.[40]

On January 13, 1784, Tyler wrote to Adams—possibly with the assistance of Mrs. Adams—that he could "no longer defer . . . soliciting the sanction of your approbation" for an engagement between himself and Nabby.[41] Adams's reply was couched in cordial terms: ". . . the testimonials I have received of your character and conduct are such as ought to remove all scruples on that head. . . . you and the young lady have my consent to arrange your plans according to your own judgments. . . ."[42] Adams also invited Tyler to make use of his law library.

Adams, however, insisted that before making final plans, his wife and daughter should meet him in London. Adams suggested that it would be "inconvenient" for Tyler to travel with the women.[43] To his wife, Adams wrote, "If the parties preserve their regard untill they meet again . . . they will still be young enough."[44] On June 20, 1784, Mrs. Adams and her daughter sailed aboard the ship *Active,* bound for England. Mrs. Adams wrote, ". . . the parting of two persons strongly attached to each other is only to be felt; discription fails."[45]

Abigail and Nabby arrived in London in August 1784 for a reunion with John Adams. The family lived briefly in a suburb of Paris. In May 1785 Adams took up residence in London as the United States' first minister to the Court of St. James. In London, Nabby met Colonel William Stephens Smith, secretary of the American legation and a protégé of George Washington.[46]

Mrs. Adams's sister, Mary Cranch, reported to the Adamses that Tyler stayed in his room for days at a time, spoke to no one, glowered, wrote rarely, but enjoyed showing off the letters he had received from Nabby. Furthermore, Mrs. Cranch declared that Tyler was failing to deliver letters that had been entrusted to him from abroad.[47] It was also reported that Tyler had gained some notoriety for ascending in a balloon, a popular new sport.[48] Tyler family tradition holds that Mrs. Cranch wrote unfavorable reports because she had earlier hoped the young lawyer would court one of her daughters.[49]

Nabby received only four letters from Tyler during the year she was in Europe.[50] Mrs. Adams commented to her sister, "A woman may forgive the man she loves an indiscretion, but never a neglect."[51] In 1785, probably in August, Nabby returned to Tyler his miniature portrait and the few letters he had written. Her accompanying statement was brief:

> Sir—Herewith you receive your letters & miniature with my desire that you would return mine to my uncle Tufts & my hopes that you are as well satisfied with the affair as is
>
> A.A.—[52]

On May 22, 1786, Mrs. Adams wrote, "I wish the Gentleman well he has good qualities, indeed he has. but he was ever his own enemy. . . ."[53] In London the romance of Nabby with Colonel William Smith was progressing. Mrs. Adams described Smith as "a

Gentleman of unblemished reputation. . . ."[54] Colonel Smith and Nabby were married on June 12, 1786.[55] Thirteen years later when John Adams was President of the United States, he wrote about William Smith, "All the actions of my life and all the conduct of my children have not yet disgraced me as much as this man. His pay will not feed his dogs; and his dogs must be fed if his children starve. What a folly!"[56]

After the engagement with Nabby had been broken, Tyler neglected his Braintree property, which eventually reverted to its original owners and later was purchased by John Adams himself. In August of 1786, Tyler handed over the Adams papers and accounts to an uncle of his former fiancée.[57] Tyler family tradition says that afer receiving Nabby's letter Tyler went into seclusion, living with his mother in Jamaica Plain. By the winter of 1786 - 87, however, Tyler was in Boston, boarding at the home of Joseph Pearse Palmer and practicing law in the city.[58]

V *An American Drama (1786 - 1787)*

In 1786 Daniel Shays, who had been commended for bravery at Bunker Hill, became the leader of a group of dissident New England farmers. Beset by numerous financial problems, including a rural depression, these farmers had begun a series of protests. They interfered with local governmental bodies, not permitting them to meet until grievances were redressed.[59] In January 1787 Governor James Bowdoin of Massachusetts declared a state of rebellion. He appointed Major General Benjamin Lincoln to suppress the rebellion. Royall Tyler became Lincoln's aide-de-camp.[60]

On one occasion, Major Tyler and his men captured a group of rebels who had gathered for Sunday services. "Waiting till the orator had concluded he [Tyler] then walked up into the pulpit, informed them [the rebels] that they were his prisoners and then went on with a long and earnest speech in refutation of the misrepresentations and calumnies agst the Gov'n't. . . ."[61] The men agreed to surrender.

Eventually, defeated by the Massachusetts forces, Shays and his chief lieutenants escaped into the Territory of Vermont, which was then claimed by New York. On February 8, 1787, the legislature of Massachusetts passed a resolution offering a reward for the rebels and requesting cooperation from neighboring states. The Vermonters would have to be persuaded to reject the rebels, while the

New Yorkers would have to be conciliated about direct dealings with a territory to which they still laid claim. General Lincoln chose Royall Tyler to negotiate with the Vermont government and to "pursue & apprehend these delinquents. . . ."[62]

On February 15, 1787, Tyler set out for Vermont. He spoke at length with various state officials.[63] He attempted to trick Shays into surrender and almost arrested the real firebrand of the rebels, Luke Day. Tyler did arrest another leader, Abram Wheeler, who later was rescued by a mob.[64]

On February 24, 1787, Governor Thomas Chittenden of Vermont issued a statement with the concurrence of the legislature. The citizens of Vermont were commanded "not to harbor, entertain or conceal" the rebels.[65] All officials were ordered to cooperate in suppressing or apprehending the insurgents. Tyler's negotiations had met with some success.

Tyler wrote to the Palmers, his friends from Braintree, about his adventures: "How I wish you could . . . see your old friend the center, the main spring of movements, that he once thought would have crazzed his brain—this minute, harranging the Governor and Council: and House of Representatives the next, driving 40 miles into the State of New York, at the head of a party to apprehend Shays . . . now, closing the passes to Canada: next writing orders to the frontier. . . . Will not this make you laugh? —I hope to be home, and bring Shays with me." Tyler asked to be remembered to the Palmers' daughter, Mary, not yet twelve years old: "Love to my little wife. Adieu."[66]

By early March, Tyler was back in Boston. On March 7, he was entrusted with another important mission. Governor Bowdoin wanted to send to New York a negotiator who was familiar with "the measures that have been taken to suppress the rebellion. . . ."[67] Armed with £30 of state money, Tyler set out. On March 12, 1787, he arrived in the city of New York. Besides gaining the state's support against Shays, Tyler appears to have indulged a taste which Boston law forbade. He went to the theater.[68] And Tyler wrote a play.

The Contrast, which opened at the John Street Theatre on April 16, 1787, was the first American comic drama to be produced professionally in the United States. Tyler followed this success by writing *May Day in Town*, presented at the John Street Theatre on May 19, 1787. Although *May Day* is no longer extant, its songs—printed as a pamphlet—have recently been discovered.[69] In

New York, Tyler "was petted, caressed, feasted and toasted, and no doubt lived too freely. . . ."[70] Soon, however, he left New York and once more secluded himself with his mother in Jamaica Plain.

VI *Another American Romance (1787 - 1792)*

In 1790 Tyler, who had returned to Boston, left his law practice and went to Vermont with the intention of moving there permanently. He also renewed his acquaintanceship with the young woman who was to become his wife, Mary Palmer.[71] Mary, the daughter of Joseph Pearse Palmer and Elizabeth Hunt Palmer had been born in 1775. Her family had lost its fortune but was still considered prominent.[72]

When Mary was eight or nine years old, she saw Tyler for the first time:

> . . .my father was going that day to Boston. I had the promise of going with him. I was dressed in a pink calico frock. . . . I was standing at the parlor window watching every carriage, hoping it would be my father coming for me. At that day it was the fashion for gentlemen to wear scarlet broadcloth coats, white vests, ruffled shirts. . . . At length a chaise with one gentleman in it drove into the yard, I could see the red coat and white vest, and my heart beating with joy. Not doubting it was my father, I ran to the door wild, with delight, but alas! quickly perceiving it was not he, I ran back disappointed. The gentleman followed immediately, and, in his cheerful musical voice, began to ask me who I expected. . . . I was astonished; his appearance, his manners, his looks overpowered me; I had never seen anything so beautiful. . . .[73]

It was Mary whom Tyler had mentioned as "my little wife" when he wrote the spirited letter from Vermont. Now that child was a young woman. In 1792, Tyler visited the Palmers in Framingham, Massachusetts, and proposed to Mary. Accepted by her, he said, "I believed there was one faithful heart in the world on whom I could rely."[74] But the marriage date was not set. Tyler was still getting settled in the new state of Vermont. Mary commented, "He said he must 'prepare a cage before he took his bird.' "[75]

VII *The Early Vermont Years (1792 - 1801)*

Tyler had moved to a fast-growing state and to its largest city, Guilford.[76] He soon became a prominent resident of Guilford. Tyler's law docket for 1793 shows an active and varied practice.[77] In

1794, Tyler and Mary were privately married.[78] The same year the people of Guilford recommended Tyler's nomination to Congress, but he was not nominated.[79] In February of 1796, Tyler brought his young wife and their first child to Vermont.[80]

The Tylers' arrival in Vermont was a special occasion. Henry Burnham, a young neighbor, recalled: "Their first coming . . . [was] the morning dawn of intellectual life in this region. . . ."[81] Another Vermont neighbor, James Elliot (later a member of Congress), wrote a poetic effusion praising Tyler's "Art, eloquence and taste. . . ."[82] In 1801 the Tylers left Guilford and moved to a farm at Brattleboro.[83] One of Tyler's poems describes the area as a "wild sweet valley. . . cradled in granite arms. . . ."[84]

Tyler's law career often took him into Walpole, New Hampshire, where he met several young men interested in law and literature. Most important among these men was Joseph Dennie.[85] Tyler and Dennie became lifelong friends. Starting in 1794, the two men wrote a popular series of essays, poems, and anecdotes which appeared under the title of Colon & Spondee.[86]

Tyler's neighbors appreciated both his cleverness and his legal skills. In 1794 Tyler was elected State's Attorney for Windham County, a position which he held until 1801.[87] A work printed in 1797 described him: "Does misery need an advocate? . . . in Mr. *Tylor* it finds a man, who . . . feels for the errors of others, pities their vices, and compassionates their wants. How commanding in his oratory. . . . with what resistless power does it assail the hearers! . . . Mr. *Tylor* is looked up to with admiration, affection, and esteem."[88]

Tyler was active as a writer during his early years in Vermont. His novel *The Algerine Captive* was published anonymously (Walpole, N.H.: David Carlisle, 1797). This two-volume work is part local color and part exotic adventure. The first volume is the story of a young man, Updike Underhill, growing up in Boston in the 1770s and 1780s. The second volume tells of Updike's capture by the Barbary pirates, his slavery in Algiers, and his eventual escape. *The Algerine Captive* was one of the earliest American novels, the first novel to describe life in New England. It was also one of the first American novels to be republished in England.[89] On October 30, 1797, the comic play *The Georgia Spec,* now lost, was performed in Boston.[90] Tyler was also a popular orator. Except for the *Oration . . . in Commemoration of the Death of General George Washington,* printed in 1800, no speech by Tyler has survived.[91]

The Tylers were firmly established in Vermont. Writing to her mother in 1800, Mary reported, "I have exceeding kind neighbors, a Good Physician, and what is better than everything else in the world, one of the tenderest, most attentive, most affectionate of husbands. . . ."[92] The Tylers would eventually have eleven children.[93] In 1800, Tyler's mother died.[94] The following year, after the settlement of Mary Whitwell's estate, the Tylers purchased and moved to a large house on a 150-acre farm at Brattleboro.[95] With the new century under way, Royall Tyler was to continue his career as a man of law and a man of letters.

VIII *Man of Law and Letters (1801 - 1813)*

One of Tyler's earliest Vermont friends, the Federalist Isaac Tichenor, was reelected governor of Vermont in 1801. That same year Tyler, also a Federalist, was elected by the Republican-dominated legislature to the Supreme Court of the State of Vermont. As Side or Assistant Judge, Tyler was paid $900 a year. The Chief Justice was paid the highest salary of any elected official in the state, $1,000. Under the old system of annual elections by the legislature, Tyler had one of the longest tenures on the Vermont court. He was elected six times as Assistant Judge and six times as Chief Justice.[96] Because the Vermont Supreme Court was a circuit court, Tyler had to spend ten months of every year on the road.

Tyler was elected a Trustee of the University of Vermont in 1802. His main service to the university appears to have been as its advocate with the legislature. Tyler helped to draw up the laws and regulations for the college (1811) and worked on the drafting of the college's charter.[97] Also in 1811, Tyler was appointed Professor of Jurisprudence, the only such appointment the University of Vermont has ever made. Later that year the university awarded Tyler an honorary Master of Arts degree. Although there is no record of his resignation, Tyler's services to the University of Vermont seem to have ended by 1814.[98]

Besides his other activities, Tyler was still writing. Some of his Colon & Spondee columns were anthologized in *The Spirit of the Farmers' Museum.*[99] In 1801, Tyler began contributing to Joseph Dennie's *Port Folio.* In 1807 and 1808, Tyler's poetry and essays appeared in Joseph T. Buckingham's *Polyanthos.* The New York publisher Isaac Riley issued Tyler's *Reports of Cases Argued and Determined in the Supreme Court of Judicature of the State of Vermont* (Volume I, 1809; Volume II, 1810). In 1809, Riley published

Tyler's book of fictional letters *The Yankey in London.*[100] Riley also published a book by Mrs. Tyler, *The Maternal Physician: A Treatise on the Nurture and Management of Infants From the Birth Until Two Years Old. Being the Result of Sixteen Years' Experience in the Nursery* (1811; second edition, 1818). This is one of America's first books of advice on infant care.[101]

In 1807, Tyler became Chief Justice of the Vermont Supreme Court. After his election as Chief Justice, Tyler seems to have changed his political preferences from Federalist to Republican.[102] As the War of 1812 approached, his correspondence reveals the inner thinking of those Americans who wanted to break the ties with England.[103] Tyler also foresaw state interposition. He realized that ". . . a state cannot be hung for a rebel. . . ." He deplored the possibility that the nation would eventually be torn apart by struggles between the states and the federal government.[104]

In 1812, Tyler ran for the United States Senate but was defeated. At that time the state legislature chose the senators. In 1813 the Federalists won power in Vermont. Tyler, now identified with the Republicans, was not reelected to the state's Supreme Court.[105] From this time forward, the good fortune of Tyler's previous years would be reversed by bereavement, poverty, sickness, pain, disfigurement, and death.

IX *The Declining Years (1813 - 1826)*

Tyler's friend and collaborator Joseph Dennie had died in 1812. Tyler suffered another severe loss in the autumn of 1813. His oldest son, Royall, Jr., who was at the university in Burlington, Vermont, died of typhoid fever.[106] Shortly afterward, the family underwent a financial crisis caused by Tyler's creditors.[107] Tyler's salary as Chief Justice had never been munificent; now there was no salary. His law practice would have to be rebuilt.[108] In 1815 the former judge and his family moved from their farm home to the town of Brattleboro. During the same year, Tyler was appointed Register of Probate for Windham County, a position in which he served until 1822.[109]

But Tyler had been too long away from his legal practice. Also, a cancerous growth was developing on his face. He gradually became incapacitated by this illness. The bleak financial situation of the former Chief Justice and the strength of character of his wife are revealed in Mary's diary. On June 10, 1822, Mary noted: "Mr Tyler went to New Fane Court—spirits low—purse still lower—only one cent in his pocket—and very little prospect of business—God in mercy remember thy Servants and help us in this time of trouble—after My Husband was gone I took up Carpets etc etc—"[110]

During those last years Tyler continued to write. He completed a comic drama, *The Island of Barrataria*, probably sometime after 1813. He contributed prose and poetry to a number of publications. He worked on a book of miscellanies to be entitled "Utile Dulci."[111] In 1824 and 1825 he completed three plays: *Joseph and His Brethren, The Judgement of Solomon*, and *The Origin of the Feast of Purim.*[112] Tyler also wrote a long and interesting poem, "The Chestnut Tree," which was first published in 1931.[113]

After the cancer affected Tyler's eyesight, he would write in large chalk letters on a slate, and Mary would copy his works into manuscript form. This was the method used in 1824 and 1825 to revise the autobiographical sections of *The Algerine Captive.* The revision, entitled *The Bay Boy,* was not published until 1972.[114] Mary wrote (May 15, 1825) to her son Edward, "At present we are busily engaged on the *Bay Boy.* . . . it needs all my art and management to induce him to go on. . . . his bodily sufferings are so great that nothing but the hope I keep alive in his brain of leaving something behind him that may be of service to his children could possibly give him courage to proceed. . . ."[115]

The agony of those final years is chronicled in Mary Palmer Tyler's diary:[116]

1822

April 14—My Husband not so well as he has been I feel anxious about him—
May 28— . . . dreadful news that our beloved John has failed in Business . . . ; May 29—My Husband—My Son—how does my heart bleed for both—

John had been his parents' main source of income for several years. After he failed in business, the Tylers were dependent upon the generosity of their other children, and of friends and neighbors. Mary took in sewing to earn money. The family was kept alive with gifts of money, fuel, and food.

Mary's diary continues:

1823

Feb. 6—My Husband very unwell for a week past and continues so—
Sept. 3— . . . no better—scarcely able to see or speak. . . .

1824

Oct. 17— . . . We began a course of medicine which has so far proved favorable—

Oct. 26—Last night my Husband had a very ill turn—

Nov. 2—My Husband very low—I cannot think his medicine of any service—

1825

Oct. 19—My Poor Husband very ill—grows weak—appetite very poor—

Oct. 23/24—Mending for self and children—reading to my Sick Husband—

1826

Jan. 20— . . . Husband very low in health and spirits—

July 3— . . . Husband took the first dose of the juice of Chivers—strongly recommended as a cure for Cancer—

July 7—Chivers made my Husband very sick.

On July 10, 1826, Mary noted in her diary the death of John Adams. On July 13, she recorded the death of Thomas Jefferson. The two former presidents had died withinn a few hours of each other on July 4, 1826. Mary's diary continues.

August 26, 1826—My beloved Husband was taken delerious [on August 7], and afterwards rapidly declined. . . . On Wednesday the 16th My Husband was released from his sufferings. . . . My Husband died with perfect composure and resignation and surely he passed from Death unto Life![117]

Royall Tyler was buried in Brattleboro, Vermont.

In 1858, Mary Tyler began to write a book of memoirs for her descendants. She recalled the first time she met Tyler: ". . . I had never seen anything so beautiful . . . you, who never saw him in his beauty, can have no idea of it. . . . if ever a life-long love was commenced at first sight, it was then done on my part. I certainly loved him then and always afterwards. . . ."[118] This was Mary's epigram for her husband—Royall Tyler, author of *The Contrast,* and a significant figure in American literature.

CHAPTER 2

The Contrast: *A First*

THE *Contrast* is a comedy of manners "WRITTEN BY A CITIZEN OF THE UNITED STATES."[1] The play opened at the John Street Theatre in New York City on April 16, 1787. *The Contrast* was the first American comedy to be produced by a company of professional actors.

I *The Writing of* The Contrast

Royall Tyler had arrived in New York City on March 12, 1787, on a mission for the government of Massachusetts.[2] In Massachusetts, theatrical entertainments were specifically forbidden by an ordinance of 1750, but New York had a thriving professional theater.[3] In New York, Royall Tyler probably saw his first professionally produced plays.[4]

It may seem surprising that Tyler, who until his New York visit "had never attended a theatrical performance,"[5] could write *The Contrast* in such a short time. But Tyler was a facile and speedy writer, as well as a voracious reader. Despite the prohibition in Boston against stage plays, surreptitious theatrical productions did take place there.[6] In *The Bay Boy*, Tyler describes a clandestine performance of Joseph Addison's *Cato* and the performance of a Christmas Mummers' Play.[7]

Some commentators believe that Tyler brought the as-yet-uncompleted *Contrast* with him when he came to New York. Tyler's great-granddaughter Helen Tyler Brown suggests that ". . . if he did not carry to New York the unfinished play in his pocket, he may have carried the idea in his mind."[8] In New York, Tyler apparently attended plays and made friends with some actors, particularly with Thomas Wignell. Wignell played the comic character of Jonathan in *The Contrast* when the play was produced by Lewis Hallam's American Company.

II *The United States' First Comic Drama:* The Contrast

A reviewer wrote, "I was present last evening at the representation of *The Contrast,* and was very much entertained with it. It is certainly the production of a man of genius. . . . the effusions of an honest patriotic heart. . . ."[9] *The Contrast* begins with a prologue, "WRITTEN BY A YOUNG GENTLEMAN OF NEW-YORK, AND SPOKEN BY MR. WIGNELL."[10] Most critics believe that Tyler wrote the prologue.[11] The speech praises "native themes" and "homespun arts" in preference to splendors imitated from Europe (pp. 20 - 21).

Act I of Tyler's comedy of manners opens with a dialogue between two flirtatious young women of New York, Charlotte Manly and her friend Letitia, an heiress. They gossip about the betrothal of Maria Van Rough to Billy Dimple. Billy had visited England and had become a fop, "a flippant, pallid, polite beau, who . . . reads a few pages of Chesterfield's letters, and then minces out, to put the infamous principles in practice. . ." (p. 27). Despite her aversion to Dimple, Maria will not terminate the engagement because she is a dutiful daughter. In an aside, Charlotte says that Dimple is secretly courting her, also.

Maria is introduced in Act I, Scene II. She is chided by her father, Van Rough, for her "doleful ditties" and for reading sentimental novels (p. 34). Van Rough, a practical businessman, warns his daughter to "keep your eye upon the main chance . . ." (p. 35).

As Act II opens, Charlotte has received word that her brother, Colonel Henry Manly, is in New York. Charlotte describes her brother as ". . . the very counterpart and reverse of me: I am gay, he is grave; I am airy, he is solid. . ." (p. 42). When Manly arrives, Charlotte teases him for his sentimental attitudes. At the end of this scene, Letitia reveals that she too is being secretly courted by Dimple.

In Scene II, Jessamy, Dimple's foppish manservant and imitator, meets Colonel Manly's rustic servant Jonathan. Prompted by Jessamy, Jonathan agrees to woo Maria's servant Jenny. Jessamy hopes that Jenny will see "the contrast . . . between the blundering Jonathan and the courtly and accomplished Jessamy!" (p. 63).

Billy Dimple is introduced in Act III, Scene I, reading from his mentor, Lord Chesterfield. Dimple plots to ". . . break with Maria, marry Letitia, and as for Charlotte—why, Charlotte must be a companion to my wife" (p. 66). After Dimple leaves, Jessamy introduces Jenny to Jonathan. The girl teases Jonathan about the play he had attended the night before, but Jonathan denies having gone to the theater for that is "the devil's drawing-room. . ." (p. 70). He says that he merely had followed some people into a building: ". . . they shewed me away, clean up to the garret, just like meeting-house gallery. . . . they lifted up a great green cloth and let us look right into the next neighbour's house" (pp. 71 - 72). The rustic goes on to describe what he saw.

Apparently, Jonathan has confused and combined John O'Keeffe's *Poor Soldier* and Richard Brinsley Sheridan's *School for Scandal* (which Tyler could have seen presented together at the John Street Theatre on March 21, 1787).[12] Jenny and Jessamy persuade Jonathan that he has been at a play. The rustic then remembers that the place "smelt tarnally of brimstone" (p. 73). The play scene is one of the best known and most amusing moments in *The Contrast.* Jessamy encourages Jonathan to woo Jenny and leaves the two alone. To entertain the girl, Jonathan sings several verses from "Yankee Doodle" (p. 76). When Jonathan becomes too forward, Jenny slaps him and runs away.

At the beginning of Act III, Scene II, Manly soliloquizes that "Luxury is surely the bane of a nation. . ." (p. 79). He extols a federal union of states (pp. 79 - 80). Meeting Dimple on the mall, Manly at first succumbs to the fop's flattery. Invited to join in some social flirtations, however, Manly responds with disapproval. Just in time, Dimple learns that Manly is Charlotte's brother.

In Act IV, Scene I, Maria describes a meeting with a boarder from a nearby residence who mistakenly "came into our house instead of his lodgings. . . ." This intruder won Maria's approval with his "genteel apology . . . so manly and noble!" (p. 87). When Dimple and Manly join the ladies, Maria realizes that it was the colonel who had "unintentionally intruded" upon her that morning (p. 90). The scene ends with Dimple planning assignations first with Letitia and then with Charlotte.

In Act IV, Scene II, Van Rough is unhappy at learning that Dimple is in debt. Hearing voices, Van Rough hides in order to eavesdrop. Manly enters with Maria and begins to court her. Engaged to Dimple, Maria foresees "days of misery" when "the man I cannot love will make me think of him whom I could prefer" (p. 99). The honorable Manly agrees that it is Maria's "duty" to obey her father. He comforts Maria with a skillfully phrased non sequitur: ". . . if we are not happy, we shall, at least, deserve to be so. Adieu!" (p. 99).

The final scene of the play (Act V, Scene II) is set in Charlotte's apartment. Tyler's indebtedness to Sheridan's "screen scene" in *The School for Scandal* is apparent here. Manly, finding no one in the apartment, takes a book into an anteroom. Dimple enters the main room with Letitia. He says that he prefers her to Maria and Charlotte. Charlotte enters, and Letitia pretends to leave but returns to listen at the door. Dimple tells Charlotte that he has no affection for Letitia. He forces a kiss upon Charlotte. When she screams, Colonel Manly rushes into the room. He and Dimple draw their swords and fight until Van Rough enters and beats down the weapons.

The angry Letitia reenters and reveals Dimple's intrigues. The fop prepares to leave, suggesting that he will challenge Manly to a duel.[13] Manly replies, "I have a cane to chastise the insolence of a scoundrel. . ." (p. 112). After Dimple leaves, Manly offers himself as a suitor for Maria. Van Rough gives his consent, advising the young man to ". . . mind the main chance. . ." (p. 113). Letitia and Charlotte apologize. Then Manly concludes the play by asking for "the applause of the PUBLIC" (p. 115).

III *An Early Declaration of Cultural Independence: Themes in* The Contrast

The Contrast is a patriotic play which urges Americans to divorce themselves from the affectations of foreign behavior. It is "a spiritual Declaration of Independence."[14] The theme of patriotism is introduced in the prologue. The play is set not in "foreign climes" but in New York. The stress is on "native themes." American writers should promote America: "Let your own Bards be proud to copy *you!*" The prologue praises the young nation's "native worth" and encourages its "homespun arts" (pp. 20 - 21).

In *The Contrast* the honorable, patriotic Manly is the antithesis of the foppish, hypocritical Dimple. Manly represents America and virtue. Dimple represents foreign customs and amorality.[15] Dimple and his servant are cunning followers of Lord Chesterfield; Manly and his servant are plain, honest Americans.

Manly frequently defends the virtues of his nation. When Dimple asks whether the colonel has travelled abroad, Manly retorts, "I can never esteem that knowledge valuable which tends to give me a distaste for my native country" (p. 92). Manly's patriotism is unswerving. His servant Jonathan explains Manly's attitude toward Shays'

Rebellion: "Colonel said that it was a burning shame . . . to have any hand in kicking up a cursed dust against a government which we had, every mother's son of us, a hand in making" (p. 56). Manly is devoted to the government and to those who helped achieve liberty. He says, "I have humbly imitated our illustrious WASHINGTON, in having exposed my health and life in the service of my country. . ."[16] (p. 47).

In *The Contrast* Royall Tyler promotes American virtues and encourages a national literature. He praises American heroes and soldiers. He preaches federal unity and fiscal responsibility. The play attacks luxury, adherence to fashions, and frivolous behavior. *The Contrast* was produced only a few weeks before the opening of the Constitutional Convention on May 25, 1787. Tyler's comedy of manners reflects attitudes that existed in the new nation.

IV *Honor and Sentiment: Maria and Manly*

Characterization is an important element in *The Contrast*. The sentimental hero and heroine, Manly and Maria, are recognizable stage types.[17] Tyler's characters apparently are borrowed from the sentimental plays and comedies of manners which dominated eighteenth-century English drama. One of the earliest reviews of *The Contrast* praises Manly, the "heroick, sentimental Colonel. . . ."[18] To another contemporary reviewer, Manly is "at once the illustrious citizen, the gallant officer, and the patriotic and political philosopher."[19] A modern critic says that Manly represents "morality, honor, and justice. . . ."[20]

Not all critics appreciate the sober colonel. A nineteenth-century writer calls Manly "a most insufferable prig."[21] A twentieth-century commentator says that Manly is "unintentionally the most humorous character of all."[22] Yet, was the humor unintentional? Perhaps Manly's tendency to overstate his thoughts is meant to be both praiseworthy and amusing. At times Manly is a typical sentimental hero; at other times he seems to be a parody of the sentimental hero. As one critic says, viewers "laugh at Manly's exaggerated seriousness while . . . [respecting] his more admirable qualities."[23]

Before Manly appears on stage, he is described by Charlotte: "His conversation is like a rich, old-fashioned brocade,—it will stand alone; every sentence is a sentiment" (p. 43). The exaggerated manner with which Manly first greets his sister illustrates the colonel's sentimentality, gravity, and effusiveness, as well as Tyler's skill at parody. Manly declares, "My dear Charlotte, I am happy that I once more enfold you within the arms of fraternal affection. I know you are going to ask (amiable impatience!) how our parents do,—the venerable pair transmit you their blessing by me. They totter on the verge of a well-spent life, and wish only to see their children settled in the world, to depart in peace" (p. 45). As the clever Charlotte says later, "Let my brother set out where he will in the fields of conversation, he is sure to end his tour in the temple of gravity" (p. 92).

Manly is more than a parody of the sentimental hero, however. The colonel also embodies the most admirable traits to be found in the American character.[24] Manly is the play's spokesman for themes of honor, patriotism, and duty. It is little wonder that Charlotte thinks of her brother as an appropriate suitor for Maria: ". . . that pair of pensorosos . . . with a flow of sentiment meandering through their conversation like purling streams in modern poetry" (p. 44).[25]

Like Manly, Maria is a combination of virtue and sentiment, at once admirable and amusing. She is exemplified in her aphorism: ". . . the only safe asylum a woman of delicacy can find is in the arms of a man of honour" (pp. 33 - 34).[26] Maria despises "the odious Dimple" (p. 87)[27] and says that his "only virtue is a polished exterior. . ." (pp. 38 - 39). She praises the stranger who blundered into her presence and ". . . entered readily into a conversation worthy a man of sense to speak, and a lady of delicacy and sentiment to hear" (p. 88). Maria and Manly are alike in their sentiment and virtue.

V *Fops, Flirts, and Men of Affairs: Dimple, Charlotte and Letitia, and Van Rough*

The Anglicized Dimple is a rogue, a hypocrite, a fop, a "*reductio ad abusurdum* of the Chesterfieldian world."[28] Mrs. John Adams thought that the depiction of Dimple was a subtle attack on Nabby Adams's husband, Colonel William Smith. Mrs. Adams wrote that she suspected Tyler was ". . . drawing his own Character and an other Gentlemans. . . ."[29]

Dimple's hypocrisy is illustrated in his flattering conversations with Manly (Act III, Scene II). Dimple's hypocrisy is further revealed when he learns that Manly is Charlotte's brother. The would-be seducer laments, "Plague on it! . . . A fighting brother is a cursed appendage to a fine girl" (p. 84). Dimple is languid and bored in manner: ". . . to a man who has travelled, there is nothing that is worthy the name of amusement to be found in this city" (p. 91). Asked if he attends the theater, Dimple replies, "I was tortured there once" (p. 91).

Dimple is a rogue. He woos Letitia for her wealth while maintaining a relationship with Charlotte for her beauty. When Dimple's roguery has been disclosed, he rationalizes, ". . . an affair of this sort can never prejudice me among the ladies; they will rather long to know what the dear creature possesses to make him so agreeable" (p. 111). In his last speech, after he has been dismissed by Van Rough and Manly, the unchastened Dimple extolls himself as "a gentleman who has read Chesterfield and received the polish of Europe. . ." (p. 112). At no point, however, is there a suggestion of treason in the portrayal of Dimple's Anglicized manners or in his disparaging attitude toward his own country. The emotions of the recent Revolutionary Period have somewhat moderated.

Dimple is a combination of two traditional stage types—the superficial, fashion-loving fop and the seductive, sensual rake.[30] Dimple is also the first character in a long line of fictional Americans who, after living abroad, become alienated and develop contempt for their native land. Such a character appears in James Nelson Barker's imitation of *The Contrast*. Barker's comedy of manners, entitled *Tears and Smiles* (1807), contrasts an American naval hero with Fluttermore, a fop.[31] Dimple has been described as "a comic ancestor of Gilbert Osmond," the shallow dilettante and fortune-hunter of Henry James's *Portrait of a Lady* (1881).[32]

Like the foppish Dimple, Charlotte and Letitia are devoted to the world of fashion, gossip, and flirtation. The girls open the play with delightful banter. Charlotte recalls walking past some men at a dance: "I faultered with one of the most bewitching false steps you ever saw. . . . Gad! how my little heart thrilled to hear the confused raptures. . ." (p. 23). Charlotte then describes her main interest: "Man! for whom we dress, walk, dance, talk, lisp, languish, and smile" (p. 24). Echoing *The School for Scandal*, Charlotte says that gossip is the purpose of her life.

Charlotte and Letitia charmingly explain to Manly the delights of flirtation. They describe manners at the theater: ". . . we torture some harmless expression into a double meaning, which the poor author never dreamt of, and then we have recourse to our fans, and then we blush, and then the gentlemen jog one another, peep under the fan, and make the prettiest remarks. . ." (pp. 49 - 50). Even Manly is amused by Charlotte's description. Despite their enjoyment of fashionable superficialities, Charlotte and Letitia are not villainesses. Eventually they reject the seductive advances of Dimple and help to disclose his perfidy.

Tyler also satirizes the stolid business type. Van Rough, Maria's father, is an amusing portrayal of the man of affairs. He is a "prototype" for similar figures in later plays and novels.[33] When Maria protests her engagement to Dimple, Van Rough sternly replies that her attitude comes from reading "trumpery" and says, ". . . it is money makes the mare go; keep your eye upon the main chance, Mary" (p. 35). He advises his daughter that happiness will come from having "a good rich husband" (p. 36).

Van Rough follows his own advice about the main chance. After he learns that Dimple is seriously in debt, the merchant decides to terminate his daughter's engagement—for financial reasons. Van Rough is also shrewd. He hides when Maria enters the room with Manly, thus learning that the two are in love. The merchant finally tells Maria and Manly, ". . . you shall have my consent immediately to be married. I'll settle my fortune on you, and go and live with you the remainder of my life" (p. 113).

As one critic has noted, Van Rough combines the traits of characters from two Sheridan plays—Sir Anthony Absolute of *The Rivals* and Sir Oliver Surface of *The School for Scandal*, as well as the traits of that epitome of American pragmatism, Benjamin Franklin.[34] In Van Rough, Tyler portrayed all that is admirable and yet worthy of satire in the mercenary man of business.

VI *Yankee Servants: Jonathan and Jessamy*

In *The Contrast* Royall Tyler created one of the most amusing, original, and influential characters in American drama. A reviewer in 1790 wrote of the play's characters, "No one is, perhaps, entirely new, except . . . Jonathan. . . ."[35] When Tyler created Jonathan, he used traditional elements and a traditional name. The name "Jonathan" was applied derisively to country bumpkins in eighteenth-century America. This name was often interchanged with another pejorative term, "Yankee Doodle." Both terms eventually became good-humored designations.[36]

Like classical comedy, American drama prior to *The Contrast* had used rural characters for humorous purposes. The anonymous author of the comic drama *The Blockheads, or the Affrighted Officer* (1776) introduced a rustic character named "Simple" who had Yankee traits. Also strikingly similar to Tyler's Jonathan is the title character in *The Adventures of Jonathan Corncob*, "Written by Himself" (London, 1787).[37] Despite similarities, *Jonathan Corncob* and *The Contrast* seem to be independent creations.

Another British work which has marked similarities to *The Contrast* is Captain Joseph Atkinson's *A Match for a Widow, or the Frolics of Fancy* (1785, revised 1786, first printed 1788).[38] Atkinson's Jonath*e*n and Tyler's Jonath*a*n are comparable in several ways. Both are servants from rustic backgrounds who are uncertain about how to proceed in a sophisticated environment. Both speak in comic dialect. Both sing verses to the tune of "Yankee Doodle." But there is no actual proof that Tyler had any knowledge of Atkinson's play. In concluding an article about the Dublin Jonath*e*n, Marston Balch states that ". . . the facts, if known, would credit full originality to the American playwright [Tyler]. . . ."[39]

Regardless of how Tyler came to create his rustic figure, Jonath*a*n was the first of a long line of popular stage Yankees. The early reviewers found Tyler's rustic a delightful figure: "In the character of Jonathan, our risible faculties are irresistibly set in motion. . . ."[40]

The "father of American drama" and its earliest historian, William Dunlap, described *The Contrast* in contradictory statements. He said, "Jonathan the First has, perhaps, not been surpassed by any of his successors."[41] But Dunlap did not like the play, and complained that "Mr. Tyler . . . thought that a Yankee character, a Jonathan, stamped the piece as American, forgetting that a clown is not the type of the nation he belongs to."[42] Over the years, other critics and historians have often reacted favorably to Tyler's stage Yankee: "the original of a line of stage-Yankees,"[43] "assuredly our own,"[44] "the most positive American character in the portraiture of the stage."[45]

Jonathan is a proud individual. He denies being Colonel Manly's servant, preferring to call himself the colonel's "waiter" (p. 54). Jonathan is the country cousin lost in the big city. Looking for a church, he goes to "Holy Ground." Jessamy, who feels superior to Jonathan and makes fun of him, explains that "holy ground" is a place of prostitution (p. 57).

Jessamy's frequent advice to Jonathan—and the rustic's misapplication of that advice—adds to the play's comedy. Jessamy, echoing Dimple's Chesterfieldian principles, tries to educate the naive Jonathan, to make him more sophisticated. Later in the play, Jessamy will try unsuccessfully to teach Jonathan how to "laugh by rule," according to Dimple's "gamut" (p. 101). It is Jessamy who suggests that Jonathan might be amused with some gallantry. "Girl huntry!" Jonathan exclaims, "I never played at that game" (p. 58). Jonathan often uses malapropisms,[46] such as his earlier reference to Shays' men as "sturgeons" rather than "insurgents" (p. 55).

Jessamy coaches Jonathan in the proper techniques of wooing, ". . . talk as much as you can about hearts, darts, flames, nectar and ambrosia. . ." (p. 60). Jonathan will say to Jenny: "Burning rivers! cooling flames! red-hot roses! pig-nuts! hasty-pudding and ambrosia!" (p. 77). While wooing Jenny, who is an early example of the soubrette, Jonathan sings some verses from "Yankee Doodle." This is the first known use on stage of the traditional lyrics.[47] The 1790 publication of *The Contrast* is the first appearance of the familiar words in print. Tyler probably used lyrics that were already part of the oral tradition. (These lyrics may have been written by Tyler's Harvard classmate Edward Bangs.[48]) After Jenny's request for a song, Jonathan sings three verses of "Yankee Doodle." He starts a fourth stanza, then stops, "No, no, . . . you would be affronted if I was to sing that. . ." (p. 76). Jonathan boasts that he knows 190 verses, but "our Tabitha at home can sing it all" (p. 77). The song had many popular verses, some of them satiric and some possibly obscene.

In *The Contrast*, Jonathan incorporates traits that will become standard for the stage Yankee: honesty, boastfulness, loyalty, practicality, shrewdness, clumsiness, naiveté, garrulousness, and a distinctive dialect. Jonathan's character is created through his word choice, including malapropisms, rural terms, "lusty hyperbole and boundless exaggeration."[49] Jonathan uses expletives: "gor," "tarnation," "tarnal," "tarnal curse and damn." He also uses expressions that even today have a taint of rustic humor: "outlandish lingo," "by jingo," "I began to smell a rat," "swamp it," and "sticks in my gizzard." With Jonathan, Tyler began an American tradition of humor through dialect, a tradition which would include the work of Mark Twain.

Jonathan is the ancestor of a vast array of rural characters, frontiersmen, and stage Yankees. His descendants bear many names. Some were called Jonathan, as was Jonathan Ploughboy in Samuel

Woodworth's *Forest Rose* (1825). Others bear such humorous sobriquets as Welcome Sobersides, Horsebeam Hemlock, Seth Sage, Seth Swap, Seth Hope, Lot Sap Sago, Deuteronomy Dutiful, Calvin Cartwheel, Hiram Hireout, Ichabod Inkling, and Gumption Cute.[50] Broadly interpreted, some of Jonathan's characteristics also can be seen in frontier types like Davy Crockett. A number of dialect commentators are descended from Jonathan, starting with Seba Smith and including Hosea Biglow, Josh Billings, and Petroleum V. Nasby.

Rustic characters won popularity for such actors as George Handel ("Yankee") Hill, Henry Placide, Denman ("Uncle Joshua") Thompson, Dan Marble, and the many actors who played Toby (a red-wigged comic rustic) in tent shows throughout rural America.[51] In the twentieth century, the stage Yankee's rural shrewdness has been portrayed in various characters on stage and screen. But first of all there was Jonathan, a comic depiction of rural America—naive, honest, shrewd, and forthright.

VII *The Death Song of Alknomook*

When Maria is first introduced in Act I, Scene II, she sings a sentimental song about the death of an Indian, the son of Alknomook.[52] The song gives rise to a literary mystery: Who wrote "The Death Song of Alknomook"? Was it original to Tyler or did he, as with "Yankee Doodle," borrow an already familiar song? Indian laments were popular in America in the late eighteenth and early nineteenth centuries.[53] Such laments often depicted the courage of the Indian faced with pain and death. Among hundreds of such songs, "The Death Song of Alknomook" has been called "the best that has survived. . . ."[54]

The use of "Alknomook" in *The Contrast* is not the first appearance of the poem. Alknomook's song was first printed in Joseph Ritson's *Select Collection of English Song* (London, 1783).[55] In January 1787, under the title of "The Death Song of a Cherokee Indian," the lyrics were printed in Matthew Carey's magazine the *American Museum*.[56] The first two editions of *Museum* have no attribution of authorship for "Alknomook," but in the third edition (with a preface dated July 20, 1790), the poem is attributed to "P. Freneau."[57] Freneau's chief biographer and editor, Fred Lewis Pattee, comments that the poem ". . . is not included in any of the poet's collections. . . . The authenticity of a poem suspected to be

Freneau's may always be gravely doubted if it is not found to be included in his collected works. . . ."[58]

Professor Arthur Hopkins Quinn, the eminent scholar, undertook some research into "The Death Song of Alknomook" on behalf of Helen Tyler Brown. Quinn concluded, "My judgment is that the song is Tyler's, simply because I see no reason to attribute it to any one else."[59] Thomas J. McKee, who edited a version of *The Contrast,* agreed.[60] Certainly Tyler had the technical skill to compose such a poem. Still, there is a question as to who wrote "The Death Song of Alknomook."

VIII The Contrast *and Style*

Royall Tyler had a sharp ear for language. But, as a review said, he used soliloquies "injudiciously."[61] For instance, after Maria sings the four quatrains of "The Death Song of Alknomook," she delivers a sixty-five-line soliloquy about such topics as "The manly virtue of courage" (pp. 32 - 34). Maria's soliloquy demonstrates her sentimentality, but the speech is too long. Manly also expresses his thoughts at great length. In Act III, Scene II, Manly has a forty-one-line soliloquy about luxury and national priorities. Tyler probably intended the audience to be mildly amused by these two sentimentalists. Nevertheless, the lengthy soliloquies interrupt the play's action.[62]

One of the contrasts in the play is the difference between the speech patterns of its various characters. There are the grave, sentimental aphorisms of Manly. There are the balanced, Chesterfieldian constructions of Dimple. There is the slangy, cliché-filled talk of Van Rough and the rural dialect of Jonathan. As one critic puts it, in *The Contrast* Tyler draws our attention "not to the unity of American speech but to its diversity."[63]

IX *Production and Printing*

The Contrast is important in American theatrical history. The first play acted in English in the New World was *Ye Bare and Ye Cubb* (1665), an amateur production. The play was written by William Darby of Virginia. Although professional theater apparently began in this country about 1703, the first drama written by an American and acted by a professional company was Thomas Godfrey's tragedy *The Prince of Parthia* (printed in 1765; one performance in Philadelphia, 1767).[64] No other drama by an American was professionally produced in this country until Royall Tyler's *The Contrast* in 1787.

There are a number of "firsts" associated with *The Contrast*. It was the first professionally produced comedy written by an American, the first professionally produced drama about American life,[65] the first American play to be produced more than once, and the first American play to be reviewed in newspapers. The success of *The Contrast* helped to make drama respectable in the United States.

The Contrast was presented five times during the 1787 New York season: on April 16 (opening night); April 18 (with alterations); May 2, "at the particular request of his excellency, Mr. [John] Hancock"; May 5 (a performance not mentioned in some listings); and May 12, "for the benefit of the unhappy sufferers by the late fire at Boston (at the particular request of the Author)." The play was produced at least once more in New York, in 1789, at the time of George Washington's inauguration.[66]

Before the end of the eighteenth century, *The Contrast* had been performed approximately fifteen times outside of New York City. *The Contrast* was performed in Baltimore; Philadelphia (as a reading by Wignell in 1790);[67] Boston (where the performance in 1792 was advertised as "A Moral Lecture in five parts");[68] Georgetown, Frederick, and Hagerstown, Maryland; Alexandria, Charleston, and Richmond, Virginia; and elsewhere.[69]

There was at least one nineteenth-century production of *The Contrast*, performed by students at the American Academy of Dramatic Arts (March 18, 1894). The play was also produced at Brattleboro, Vermont, in 1912; in Boston and Philadelphia in 1917; at Cornell University in 1925; and at Columbia University in 1927.[70] Sketches from the play were presented at the Little Theatre in New York in 1933.[71] On December 12, 1954, the television program "Omnibus" produced *The Contrast*.[72] In 1957 *The Contrast* was the subject of the first program of a radio series entitled *America on Stage*. The American Theatre Company of New York included the play in its 1971 - 72 season.[73]

In 1972 the play had a revival in New York City as a musical comedy—adapted by Anthony Stimac with music by Don Pippin and lyrics by Steve Brown. This musical version was also performed on March 15 - 19, 1974, as part of the opening ceremonies for the Royall Tyler Theatre at the University of Vermont. There were

Bicentennial performances of the play in 1976, including productions in Loudonville, New York; at Hamline University, the University of Akron, the University of Minnesota, and at the John Drew Theater in East Hampton, New York. The GeVa Company of Rochester, New York, presented the play in 1976 in Rochester and at the Edinburgh Fringe Festival.[74]

In its initial printing of 1790 (Philadelphia: Prichard and Hall), *The Contrast* made history. Tyler had assigned the rights to Thomas Wignell, who proposed a subscription printing. Wignell stipulated that the work would be issued in octavo, with an engraving by an American artist, at the price of half a dollar per copy.[75] The engraving was done by William Dunlap, who later became an important American playwright. The printing attracted subscribers from the major cities of the new nation as well as from Jamaica, Madeira, Barbados, and London. There were 658 copies subscribed to by 371 people, including Colonel David Humphreys, Aaron Burr, Major General Baron Stuben, Edmund Randolph, and Robert Morris. Heading the list of subscribers was George Washington, the President of the United States.[76]

By the middle years of the nineteenth century, all printed copies of *The Contrast* had apparently disappeared. The book collector L. E. Chittenden began searching for a copy. In 1876 Chittenden discovered *The Contrast* listed in a catalog of Washingtonia.[77] Thus, the nation's first professionally produced comedy came to light in the copy owned and autographed by the nation's first president.[78] There are now in existence about thirteen copies of the original printing of *The Contrast*.[79] The play, which is widely anthologized, is also available in the Wilbur edition of 1920 and in a 1970 reproduction of the Wilbur edition.

X *Critical Reactions to* The Contrast

Contemporary reviews of *The Contrast* were generally favorable. The earliest review seems to be the one by Candour (*Daily Advertiser*, April 18, 1787). This is the first review of an American play. Candour praises *The Contrast* but criticizes the soliloquies, Wignell's "pronunciation," the "want of interest and plot," and the author's lack of appreciation for Lord Chesterfield. Nevertheless, Candour concludes that the play ". . . does the greatest credit to the author, and must give pleasure to the spectator."[80]

The reviewer in the *New York Independent Journal* (May 5,

1787) said the play was "an extraordinary effort of genius. . . . America may one day rank a Tyler in the Dramatic Line as she already does a Franklin and a West in those of Philosophy and the Fine Arts."[81] The *Maryland Gazette or, the Baltimore Advertiser* (November 13, 1787) said that the play rivaled "the most celebrated productions of the British muse. . . ."[82] The *Maryland Journal* (November 16, 1787) described the production as a "lively Effort of American Dramatic Genius . . ." and called Tyler an "ingenious Author. . . ."[83] The *Worcester Magazine* (May 1787) reported that the play received "continued roars of applause. . . ."[84]

In 1794, Judith Sargent Murray published an "Occasional Epilogue to the Contrast; a Comedy written by Royal Tyler, Esq." In this highly complimentary work, Mrs. Murray says, ". . . taste, and sense, and reason must admire; / The Contrast . . ." and she praises Tyler as "This universal genius. . . ."[85] On the other hand, the playwright and stage historian William Dunlap said that the play was "extremely deficient in plot, dialogue, or incident. . . ."[86] Some later critics have also been unfavorable. George Seilhamer says that *The Contrast* betrays ". . . the author's want of familiarity with theatrical methods."[87] In direct opposition, Arthur H. Nethercot says, ". . . Tyler knew the rules [of drama] *too* well and followed them *too* closely to produce a really natural and original work."[88] Montrose J. Moses calls the play a "poor copy of Sheridan."[89]

Other modern critics are kinder. Arthur Hobson Quinn says that the play reads well and states that it "actually comes to life upon the stage."[90] Constance Rourke agrees that the play "reads and acts more than passably well. . . ."[91] Van Wyck Brooks says that the play is "Lively, witty, and real. . . ."[92] Theodore Hornberger describes Tyler as probably "The most sophisticated of the early portrayers of American types. . . ."[93]

The Anthony Stimac musical version of *The Contrast* was reviewed in 1972 by three New York critics. Clive Barnes suggests that ". . .Tyler was better than Mr. Stimac" and calls the play an "18th-century, all American spoof. . . ."[94] Harold Clurman compliments the modern version, which ". . . retains the line of the original and thus preserves its spirit."[95] Walter Kerr mentions Tyler's ". . . aptitude for sly rhetoric. . . ."[96]

The Contrast is important to the history of American drama. In this play, Tyler displays a facile mind, ready humor, and the ability to master the techniques of drama. *The Contrast* is an exuberant and buoyant comedy of manners which has not lost its appeal in the twentieth century. Royall Tyler's cultural Declaration of Independence started the young nation on the road to maturity in drama.

CHAPTER 3

Tyler's Other Plays

SEVERAL of Royall Tyler's plays were produced during his lifetime but are no longer extant. Two of Tyler's produced but now lost plays, *May Day in Town* and *The Georgia Spec*, can be described in some detail. There are three other produced but now lost plays variously attributed to Tyler—*The Medium, The Mock Doctor*, and *The Farm House*. Tyler wrote four plays which were not performed during his lifetime but which are extant: *The Island of Barrataria, Joseph and His Brethren, The Judgement of Solomon*, and *The Origin of the Feast of Purim*. Among the Tyler papers there are also a few brief dramatic fragments.

I May Day in Town *and Other Lost Plays*

Tyler's *May Day in Town, or New York in an Uproar*, may be the first American comic opera. It was presented at the John Street Theatre on May 19, 1787, along with George Farquhar's *The Recruiting Officer*.[1] Mary Palmer Tyler says that *May Day* ". . . was brought out as an afterpiece with unusual success."[2] Other accounts differ. Congressman William H. Grayson described the play to James Madison: "We have lately had a new farce wrote by Poet Tyler, called May day. It has plott and incident and is as good as several of the English farces; It has however not succeeded well, owing, I believe, to ye author's making his principal character a scold. . . ."[3] George Seilhamer says that the play was "a skit on . . . the much dreaded May-movings."[4]

For *May Day*, Tyler apparently wrote original lyrics which were set to familiar tunes.[5] In 1974, Ms. Katherine Jarvis discovered the lyrics of *May Day*, "the songs that were advertised as being for sale the evening of the performance."[6] The plot of the comic opera can be partially reconstructed from the Grayson letter and the songs. In

May Day, Mr. Surdus suffers "the Plagues of a clamorous Wife" (p. 192)—apparently the "scold" referred to in the Grayson letter. The slave Pompey relates how Mrs. Surdus "rave, scol, and tomp, / She lecture ole Massa, and fly at poor Pomp . . ." (p. 193). Pompey may be the first black character to appear in an American play.[7]

Despite the Surdus's opposition, their daughter Hetty is wooed by the penniless Plantain. Hetty sings, "The Love that in Wealth was thy Joy, / Shall bless thee in Poverty too" (p. 193). In Act II, Hetty's confidante and servant sings of the beauties of May and the pleasures of the countryside, which she compares to town with its "migrating Bedsteads . . ." (p. 195). In the next song, Pompey provides further comedy:

> When Massa cross and Misse glum
> And Misse ring her larum Tongue,
> See how Pompey drive of Care,
> With ha, ha, ha! ha! ha! &c. (p. 196)

The play also features a rugged sea captain, Bowling, who has "a manly, generous Heart" (p. 196).

The finale features the Surduses, Hetty, Plantain, Captain Bowling, and Pompey. Apparently, the Surduses have withdrawn their objections to the marriage. The young couple raise their voices in joint song: "While City Folks are moving, / Love makes his Home within our Hearts, / Never more removing" (p. 197). Although it may have been America's first comic opera, *May Day in Town* does not appear to be a distinguished work. There is no indication that *May Day* had more than one performance.

George O. Seilhamer attributes to Tyler a play called *The Medium, or Happy Tea-Party* "(written by a citizen of the United States)."[8] *The Medium* played at the Federal Street Theatre in Boston on March 2, 1795. Arthur Hobson Quinn and G. Thomas Tanselle attribute the play to Judith Sargent Murray.[9] Tyler is also said to have written an adaptation of Molière's *Doctor in Spite of Himself*. Marius B. Péladeau believes that Tyler rather than Henry Fielding wrote *The Mock Doctor* that was produced in Boston on February 3, 1796.[10] This play is not extant.

Another play attributed to Tyler is *The Farm House, or The Female Duellists*. This play was announced as an afterpiece for May 6, 1796, at the Federal Street Theatre in Boston. *The Farm House* may have been an adaptation by Tyler of an English play of the same title by John Philip Kemble.[11] A news clipping from 1892 says, "Among Col. Tyler's papers has been found a fragment indorsed 'Original Manuscript of The Duelists,' a farce in three acts, as performed at the Boston theatre in 1767. . . ."[12] Helen Tyler Brown later corrected the date to 1796.[13] Thomas Pickman Tyler states that the play was "especially popular."[14] No other information is available.

Royall Tyler also wrote a play about the Yazoo land scandals in Georgia. An announcement in the *Independent Chronicle* (October 30, 1797) described "an original national DRAMA, in three acts . . . entitled *The Georgia SPEC; Or, Land in the Moon.* Written by R. Tyler, Esq. Author of the Contrast, &c."[15] This is one of the few times that Tyler's name was attached to his work. The play was performed at Boston's Haymarket Theatre on October 30, 1797. There were also three presentations at the John Street Theatre in New York (December 20 and 23, 1797, and February 12, 1798). The New York productions were under the title of *A Good Spec: Land in the Moon, or the Yankee turn'd Duelist.*[16]

The Georgia Spec was described by a contemporary writer: "It contains a rich diversity of national character and national humour, scarcely to be found in any other drama in the language. . . ."[17] No copies of *The Georgia Spec* are known to be extant.

Tyler does not seem to have written any other stage plays that were produced during his lifetime. He also wrote four plays which were not produced during his lifetime, but which were printed in the twentieth century. These are *The Island of Barrataria* and three sacred dramas—*Joseph and His Brethren, The Judgement of Solomon,* and *The Origin of the Feast of Purim.*

II The Island of Barrataria

The story of how Don Quixote's faithful follower Sancho Panza becomes the governor of Barrataria is told in Chapters 42 - 53 of Cervantes' novel.[18] In adapting the story into *The Island of Barrataria,* "a Farce in Three Acts . . . by a Bostonian," Tyler comments, ". . . the Author is informed there is a farce in print—on the same subject. . . ."[19] Tyler may be referrring to Frederick Pilon's adaptation of Thomas D'Urfey's farce *Barrataria; or Sancho Turn'd Governour.*[20]

In Tyler's play, Carlos is in love with Julietta, but her father Alvarez objects. Alvarez wants his daughter to marry "a nobleman."

Carlos replies with a typical Tyler sentiment: ". . . a man of liberal education is equal to any grandee" (p. 4). But Alvarez is adamant.

In Act One, Scene Four, the new governor—Sancho Panza—makes a triumphant entry into Barrataria. Ravenously hungry, Sancho is promised a banquet. In Act Two, Scene Two, Sancho complains that being governor is "all honour and no porridge" (p. 13). Alvarez offers the governor his daughter in marriage. Hearing about Julietta's dowry, Sancho wishes that he were not already married (p. 14).

Alvarez counsels Sancho regarding his wife, "Josephine her my Lord" (p. 14). A few lines later, Alvarez describes ". . . a mighty emperor who cast away his old wife and got a young one. . ." (p. 15). (These apparent references to Napoleon and Josephine assist in dating the composition of the play. In 1809, the Emperor Napoleon announced his divorce from his wife Josephine. The proceedings were completed in 1810.) Alvarez gives Sancho a ring and a promise, ". . .whoever demands my daughter with this ring shall have her. . ." (p. 15).

In Act Two, Scene Three, Sancho is sitting as the judge at a High Court of Justice. Unlike the episodes about the lovers, this court scene makes direct use of material from Cervantes. In one case, Sancho asks to be told the situation simply. He is advised that this would be "against all precident." Sancho replies, "President?—I never knew but one good President in my life & he is gone to glory" (p. 17). This apparent reference to George Washington, who died in 1799, also assists in dating the play.

After Sancho has pronounced comic judgment on several cases, Julietta enters, disguised as an old woman. She says that her husband is threatening to divorce her and to marry someone younger. Sancho forbids the divorce and gives the old woman Alvarez's ring.

The third act finds the famished Sancho at last escorted to his banquet. This lively scene is similar to one in Cervantes. Every time that Sancho starts to eat, the food is made to disappear. Finally the court physician explains that his duty is to insure that the governors "eat nothing injurious" (p. 24). Sancho comments, "Always suspected doctors hated ducks—sensible bird, has a good appetite, never takes physick and cries quack . . ." (p. 24).

In Act Three, Scene Two, Sancho is told of an invasion. He must put himself "at the head of the militia and fight. . ." (p. 27). Sancho responds, "I know no enemy but hunger. If the Island were invaded by a squadron of dumplings, I'd fight like a Yankee Commodore and take the whole fleet" (p. 29). This apparent reference to Commodore Oliver H. Perry is another clue to the play's date of composition. Perry won the Battle of Lake Erie in 1813.

Julietta enters, disguised as a gypsy. She presents the ring to Carlos, telling him that Alvarez has promised to give his daughter in marriage to whoever has the ring. Carlos gives the ring to Alvarez. Alvarez keeps his word. Julietta and Carlos may marry.

Suddenly a messenger enters to say that the enemy is near. In a scene taken directly from Cervantes, Sancho is bound between two large shields so that he cannot move. When the governor tries to run, he topples over and is trampled underfoot by his own soldiers (pp. 29 - 30). A captain of militia declares, ". . . the enemy are repulsed; . . . conquered by the valiant arm of the most courageous Sancho!" (p. 30). Sancho then ends the farce on a somewhat serious note: "I have for some time suspected I was the fool of the play . . . but as simple as I am, I have mother wit enough to find out in a brief day that I am unfit for office. But are there not some who govern it for years—bear abuse on abuse and have not wit enough to see that they are the Sancho's of the political play?" (p. 30).

The Island of Barrataria has energy and spirit. Although the love story which Tyler added to Cervantes is not particularly brilliant, the "enchanting playfulness" (p. 7) of Julietta is attractive. The scenes with Sancho demonstrate Tyler's sense of humor and his ability as an adaptor. The play humorously demonstrates the quibbles, the jargon, and the formalities of the legal profession. The play also makes several satiric comments about medicine and politics. One of the characters says, "As for myself I shall be silent—as I hold a good fat office—and don't wish to offend—the '*Ins* or the *Outs*'. . ." (p. 5). In 1813, Tyler himself was caught between political Ins and Outs—the Federalists and the Republicans.

The date of *The Island of Barrataria* has not been definitely established, but there are some clues in the play itself: the apparent references to the death of Washington, to Napoleon's divorce, and to Commodore Perry's victory. A partially obscured date at the bottom of several pages of the manuscript indicates that the manuscript was copied during or after 1813.[21]

Tyler's adaptation of the Barrataria sequences from Cervantes shows that he has not lost the essential skill as a dramatist which he demonstrated in *The Contrast*. Tyler chooses the best scenes from his source, gives them dramatic unity, and writes with an awareness of their farcical qualities. *The Island of Barrataria* is a delightful play that, with judicious editing and production, could still entertain a modern audience.

III Joseph and His Brethren

On January 19, 1825, Mary Palmer Tyler wrote a letter to her daughter Amelia mentioning that Tyler had ". . . finished two Sacred Dramas and is now writing the third—the first is entitled Joseph & his Brethren—the Second Solomons Judgement. . . ."[22] Mary's letter seems to provide a reliable date for *Joseph and His Brethren.* Arthur Peach and George F. Newbrough, the editors of the printed version of *Joseph,* explain: "The original manuscript of this play has not as yet been found. Our text is based . . . upon what seems to be a carefully made copy of the original script" (p. 63).[23]

All three sacred dramas demonstrate Tyler's extensive familiarity with the Bible. The source of Tyler's plot for *Joseph* is Genesis, Chapters 37 to 45. There are also a number of other biblical allusions. The play opens with a scene between two of Leah's sons—Simeon and Levi—and Rachel's older son, Joseph. Joseph is insensitive to the hostility of his half-brothers. He insists on telling them about a dream in which the sheaves of grain cut by his brothers bow to his sheaf. The brothers mock the boy.

Alone, Joseph ponders his dreams, prays that he may aid God's "mighty work," and says ". . . let me compose my erring mind / And to his righteous will be all resigned" (p. 70). This scene concludes with one of the few instances of end rhyme in the predominantly blank verse of the sacred dramas.

In the second scene, Simeon and Levi express to their oldest brother, Reuben, their violent hatred of Joseph. The horrified Reuben advises moderation. When Joseph approaches, the other brothers enter and threaten to kill him. Reuben suggests putting the lad into a pit until they decide what to do.

Scene Three begins with Reuben wondering how to free Joseph, but Simeon and Levi already have sold the boy as a slave. To explain to Jacob his son's disappearance, the brothers have slain a kid and dipped Joseph's multi-colored coat into the blood. In the fourth scene, the brothers show Jacob the bloodied coat. Jacob mourns the loss of his beloved son.

Act Two, Scene One, takes place in Egypt some years later.

Joseph has become the trusted overseer of the grain, and the brothers have come from Canaan to buy food. Joseph questions his unsuspecting brothers about their father, and then accuses the brothers of being spies. He demands that they bring to him their youngest brother, Benjamin. Simeon is detained as a hostage. Alone, Joseph speaks sentimentally about "Fraternal love" (p. 82).

In Act Two, Scene Two, Jacob reluctantly agrees to send Benjamin to Egypt. There, after the brothers have purchased corn, Joseph instructs his steward to hide a silver cup in Benjamin's sack. The steward does so and then accuses the brothers of stealing Joseph's silver cup. Jacob's sons must return to Egypt.

The sixth scene of Act Three takes place in Joseph's palace. Joseph threatens to detain Benjamin. When Judah pleads for mercy, Joseph can restrain himself no longer. Sending the Egyptians away, he reveals to the brothers his true identity. He reassures them, ". . . . Providence it was that sent me here / And you but the mere passive instruments / By which God wrought" (p. 91). Joseph wants his father told of "all my glory" and brought to Egypt (p. 93).

In the final scene of the play (Act Two, Scene Seven), the failing Jacob awaits the return of his sons. Levi, Simeon, and Reuben enter. Their disclosure is almost ludicrously abrupt.

> Levi. Peace be to you, my Father.
> Jacob. Say where is Benjamin?
> Levi. Joseph is yet alive in Egypt. (p. 95)

The old man swoons but is soon revived and reassured by Reuben. Jacob expresses his happiness in lines similar to Genesis 45:28, "It is enough / It is enough. Joseph my son, is yet alive / And I will go and see him ere I die!" (p. 95). A final Chorus, in blank verse except for one couplet, admonishes the audience to learn "to honor God," who "governs still / Human events. . ." (pp. 95 - 96).

One line may provide a clue to Tyler's intentions for his sacred dramas. The first chorus refers to "our mean Scholastic Stage . . ." (p. 78). Perhaps Tyler hoped to see the play presented by a school or university. He had already written (*c.* 1824) a skit for schoolchildren, "The Tale of Five Pumpkins." In 1825, Mary Palmer Tyler wrote about the sacred dramas, "This volumn is to be printed . . . for children—for representation at Schools. . . ."[24]

Among the sacred dramas, *Joseph and His Brethren* is the longest, with approximately 1,100 lines, excluding stage directions. It has the strongest elements of a quality which Tyler both satirized and possessed—sentimentalism. The play portrays the faith of Joseph, the jealousies among the brothers, and the paternal emotions of Jacob for his sons. Tyler adapted some of the best scenes from his source, but the play is not without defects. Its impact is diminished by the long time span to be covered, by the failure to display on stage such dramatic moments as the sale of young Joseph by his brothers, and by excessively long speeches.

Characterization is one of the more effective elements in the play. Tyler makes the brothers individuals. Levi is bitter and intemperate toward Joseph. Simeon also hates Joseph, but is mocking and sarcastic. Reuben and Judah are more temperate. At first, Joseph is exactly what the brothers describe: a "dreamer," a "fond babbler" (pp. 66 - 67). He is unaware of the effect he has on his half-brothers, whose cruel behavior is motivated by Joseph's lack of perception.

When Joseph is seized by the brothers, he says, "My trust is in the living God . . ." (p. 73). This statement of resignation is one of the play's themes and is echoed in the final lines. Joseph is also, like Tyler's earlier hero Manly, given to sentimental effusions. Joseph praises fraternal love and yearns to identify himself to his "brethren dear" (p. 85).

Jacob is portrayed as a sentimental and doting old man whose fondness for Joseph angers his other children. In some of the finest poetry in the play, Jacob mourns for his son:

> How oft has my delighted spirit seen
> My darling child like to a fruitful bough
> Watered by some pure well, shoot o'er the wall
> Its spreading branch clust'ring with precious fruit.
> Now shoot and branch and fruit forever gone—. . . . (p. 77)

Jacob's sorrow may suggest how Tyler had felt when his son Royall, Jr., died.

Tyler's adaptation of the biblical story contains well-motivated characters and some effective poetry. In *Joseph and His Brethren*, the first of the sacred dramas, Tyler demonstrates his ability to select materials for dramatic impact.

IV The Judgement of Solomon

Mary Palmer Tyler's letter of January 19, 1825, also provides the date for "Solomons Judgement—between the two Harlots. . . ." Mary says the play is ". . . quite a splendid thing. . . ."[25] *The Judgement of Solomon* is the shortest of Tyler's sacred dramas, containing about 750 lines. It follows the biblical story, mainly from I Kings 3:16 - 28, which describes the testimony before Solomon of the two unnamed harlots and gives the king's judgment. Tyler includes material and echoes from other biblical sources, especially the accounts of Solomon and Sheba found in I Kings and II Chronicles. Tyler also adds some new characters.

The two-act play begins with a prologue written in blank verse. The ideas in the last eleven lines of the prologue are similar to the ideas in Colonel Manly's speech about luxury at the beginning of Act III, Scene II, of *The Contrast*. The first scene of *Judgement* establishes a framework. Chalcol, just returned from a long trip, is greeted by another elder, Baanah, who explains about Solomon's wisdom, "the special gift of God" (p. 103).[26] Baanah describes how Solomon had a dream in which God promised him a gift, and Solomon requested ". . . an understanding heart to judge / Thy people . . ." (p. 103; See I Kings 3:9, 11 - 14).

Scene Two establishes the central conflict of the play, the dispute between two harlots, both of whom claim the same child. When Lernah claims the infant, Maachah responds, ". . . overcharg'd with wine and savory meats / You overlaid your child. . ." (p. 105). Lernah nevertheless insists that the child is hers. The two women agree to go before the judgment seat of Solomon. In this scene, sympathy for Lernah is evoked subtly by the portrayal of Maachah as a cruel worshiper of heathen gods.

Act Two, Scene One, takes place in the court of Solomon, where the Queen of Sheba has just arrived. Solomon tells her that his judgment comes from "God, the giver of all wisdom. . ." (p. 113). The elders Baanah and Chalcol are spectators, serving as a chorus. Chalcol comments: ". . . this humble trust in Israel's God / Is far more brilliant in a wise man's sight / Than all the jewels which resplendent shine. . ." (p. 113). These lines repeat the play's main theme, which was first expressed in the prologue.

The elders serve as a friendly chorus; two other characters—Shimei and Liba—act as hostile commentators. (The story of Shimei is told in I Kings 2:36 - 44.) This use of two pairs of commentators adds to the dramatic power of the courtroom scene.

Solomon hears the case of the two women. First, Lernah humbly says that the child is hers and pleads for justice. Maachah denies the story, harshly claiming that the child is hers. Informed of the lack of material evidence, Solomon orders that the ". . . disputed child / Shall now divided be in pieces twain / And on each claimant half shall be bestow'd" (p. 117). Shimei's comment, "how monstrous," indicates the shocked response of the onlookers. The cruel Maachah agrees to the judgment.

When the Armour Bearer lifts his sword, Lernah rushes forward and seizes the weapon: "Mercy, O King—let him not slay the child! / I yield unto this woman all my right" (p. 118). Solomon reveals that his decison was actually a ruse. He orders the baby to be given to Lernah and admonishes her to ". . . sin no more" (p. 118). Maachah is banished.

The Queen of Sheba ends the play with praise for Solomon:

> The temple thou has built, its golden courts
> The gate call'd beautiful, the fretted roof,
> The spacious dome, the lofty pinnacles,
> Must all decay; such is the certain doom
> Of all man's works. But I this day have seen
> A richer temple built by God's own hand
> Which shall endure when things on earth
> All pass away. . . .
> For God's own Temple is a pious heart. (pp. 119 - 20)

In one of his last works, written while he was going blind and slowly dying, Tyler thus concludes with a statement that may indicate his religious belief.

The blank verse of the epilogue repeats the play's main theme:

> And when thy mind is darken'd and no ray
> Of light and life beams on thy troubled soul,
> Then copy Israel's King, and ask of God
> Like Solomon, that He would on thee bestow
> The gift of wisdom. . . .

The epilogue's last two lines are taken almost exactly from the Sermon on the Mount (Matthew 6:29): "And unto you I say that Solomon / In all his glory was not so array'd" (p. 121).

The Judgement of Solomon is a drama of uncertain merit. One critic says that to produce it on stage would be "utterly ridiculous. . . ."[27] The play was competently produced in a readers' workshop by students at the University of Vermont on March 20 and 21, 1974. A full acting version with setting and costumes might result in an attractive spectacle, especially in the scenes at Solomon's palace. Yet it is as poetry rather than as drama that the play achieves some success.

V The Origin of the Feast of Purim

Mary Tyler's letter of January 19, 1825, says that her husband has completed two sacred dramas and "is now writing the third."[28] This letter helps to date *The Origin of the Feast of Purim.* Tyler may have considered including the 1,050-line play in "Utile Dulci," a collection of his miscellaneous writings. The reverse side of the title page to *The Origin of the Feast of Purim* contains an "Introduction to the Sacred Dramas."[29] The introduction expresses one of Tyler's favorite topics, the need for Americans to write their own literature. Tyler stresses that his plays are "HOMESPUN."[30]

In plot and dialogue, *The Origin of the Feast of Purim* is close to the story related in the Old Testament's Book of Esther. The play begins with predominantly blank-verse speeches which alternate between a chorus of men and a chorus of women. The choral dirges tell of the destruction of the First Temple and the expulsion of the Jews into Babylon in the sixth century B.C. These dirges are similar to Psalm 137.

In the second scene, Mordecai tells how King Ahasuerus prefers the beautiful Esther, Mordecai's niece, to the defiant Queen Vashti. A procession approaches with people bowing before Haman, "The King's new favourite. . ." (p. 40).[31] But Mordecai will not bow. Although this scene contains no explicit stage directions, it could be staged as a spectacle and as a confrontation between Mordecai and Haman. Haman is furious. Privately, he promises to sacrifice a living infant to his god Molock in return for revenge upon the Jews (p. 42). As in *The Judgement of Solomon,* the villain in this play is a worshiper of heathen gods.

In Act Two, Scene One, Mordecai sends a messenger to Esther with information that all the Jews are to be killed. Mordecai asks that his niece plead for the king's mercy. Esther, however, is forbidden to come into the presence of the king without his command. Mordecai tells the messenger to exhort the queen "to be / The savior of a nation. . ." (p. 45). Esther sends back a request for the Jews to fast and pray for three days. Then she will go to the king. Faithful to his biblical source, Tyler is expository rather than dramatic. Esther's off-stage reactions are described, not acted out. Unfortunately, dramatic tension is lost in the shuttling back and forth of the messenger.

In Act Two, Scene Two, Haman boasts to his wife Geresh that he is the king's favorite. He describes the scene in which Esther dared to approach the king. When Ahasuerus saw her, "his every look was love. . ." (p. 47). Haman reveals that his happiness is still clouded by the image of Mordecai, so Geresh encourages her husband to ask the king to have Mordecai hanged.

Act Three takes place at court. Ahasuerus poetically describes his sleepless night:

> The dying cadence of the distant lute
> The fall of water from the marble fonts,
> And every soothing sound was tri'd in vain
> To lull my weary spirit to repose.[32] (p. 50)

Unable to sleep, Ahasuerus had ordered the chronicles of the kingdom to be read to him. The king was thus reminded that Mordecai had once warned Esther about a plot against Ahasuerus. Ahasuerus decides to honor his benefactor and asks Haman to suggest a method. Haman, thinking that he is the one to be honored, recommends that the man should ride through the city on the king's horse, led by a noble prince. The king agrees and orders Haman to lead Mordecai in this manner. Haman dares not disobey.

In Act Three, Scene Two, Haman is summoned to the queen's banquet. Haman is pleased and in return promises to Moloch "many a fair living sacrifice. . ." (p. 56). In Scene Three, Esther prays to God for help, "Be, O God, my strength and stay!" (p. 58). The contrast between the prayers of Haman and of Esther is significant.

The banquet (Act Three, Scene Four) is the last scene of the play. The king is angry when he learns that Haman's plot against the Jews threatens Esther's safety. Haman kneels, asking Esther for mercy. The queen, however, is inflexible, and the king orders Haman to be hanged on the gallows that had been built for Mordecai.

The final speech of the play is in part a choral echo of Psalm 66: "O make a joyful noise unto the Lord / Rejoice ye in the God of our salvation. . ." (p. 60). The two choruses then end the play with lines taken from the the Book of Esther: "Let the feast of Pur be a day of joy, / The month of Adar a season of gladness! . . ." (p. 61).

In *The Origin of the Feast of Purim*, Tyler misses several opportunities for rendering the scenes dramatically. He does not put on stage the procession during which Haman is angered by Mordecai (Act One, Scene Two). In Act Two, the distress of Queen Esther and her approach to the king are described rather than dramatized. The same is true of Haman's humiliation while leading Mordecai through the streets as the man whom the king desires to honor. In the banquet scene, Haman sits silently while Esther tells the king about the courtier's treachery. Some effort on Haman's part to distract the king or to justify himself would have heightened the drama. Instead, Haman has only one line, "O mercy, mercy, my most injur'd Queen!" (p. 59). The play is often telegraphic. It fails to dramatize the compressed narrative of its biblical source.

However, the character of Haman and his vengeful personality are successfully depicted. The courtier's first lines reveal the dark nature of his soul. He has "a wounded spirit. . ." (p. 40). Haman's cruelty and his offerings of living sacrifices add power to the play.

The Origin of the Feast of Purim is written in ". . .blank verse of a flexible and at times distinguished quality."[33] For example, rich and sensuous language is used by Mordecai to describe the couches at a palace feast: ". . . canopied with curtains richly wrought / With white and blue and green—upheld by / Silver rings in marble Pillars fixed. . ." (p. 39; see Esther 1:5 - 7). A light and delicate moment is the king's description of "slumber vainly sought. . ." (p. 50). Similarly, Esther describes the preparations for the banquet with sensual images that convey the elegance of the occasion:

> . . . Do all the fountains freely cast
> Their silv'ry spray? Are the marble pavements
> Sprinkled with fragrant waters? the tapestry
> Perfumed? the royal couch arrang'd? (p. 56)

Tyler the poet is better served by *The Origin of the Feast of Purim* than is Tyler the dramatist.

VI *Fragments*

Among the Tyler papers are two fragments which appear to be parts of dramas. One is mentioned in Mary Tyler's diary (December 14, 1824): "My husband began writing a Drama for Miss Peck's School—called Five Pumpkins."[34] Thomas Pickman Tyler was a student in Miss Peck's school at the time. "The Tale of Five Pumpkins" (*c.* 1824) exists in two versions. One is a narrative; the other lists the speakers as in a drama. Tyler's short playlet is about gossip. It demonstrates how a story can grow each time that it is told.[35]

The second fragment is a 114-line dialogue between the Roman

Emperor Julian, often called "the apostate," and his Christian friend, the general Antonius. Because Antonius will not be turned from his devotions, Julian condemns him to death.[36] These poetic fragments suggest Tyler's continuing interest in moral concepts presented in dramatic form.

By adopting Vermont as a home, Tyler removed himself from opportunities to attend and to participate in theater. His later plays do not demonstrate the same skill as does *The Contrast*. But Tyler's other plays are of more than historical interest. In *The Island of Barrataria* he has created a lively and enjoyable farce. The three sacred dramas, for all their faults, reveal Tyler's poetic abilities. Rightly enough, however, Royall Tyler's fame as a dramatist rests on *The Contrast*.

CHAPTER 4

The Algerine Captive *and* The Bay Boy: *Local and Exotic Color*

IN 1797, *The Algerine Captive* was published by David Carlisle of Walpole, New Hampshire. "The celebrated new Novel, said to be written by Royall Tyler" sold for "1.50 cents."[1] Volume I describes the youthful experiences of Updike Underhill, mainly in New England. Volume II describes Underhill's adventures as a prisoner of the Algerian pirates.

Mary Tyler reports that her husband ". . . was in the habit of reading it *[The Algerine Captive]*, as he finished the chapters, to an old woman who lived with us as maid of all work. . . ." The old woman said of Underhill, " 'I do hope he will come here while I stay; do you think he will?' 'It is quite doubtful,' said your father. . . . [Years afterward] She asked us seriously if Dr. Underhill ever came to visit us."[2]

I *Background of the Novel*

In the 1790s the problems that the United States was having with the Algerian pirates had aroused great public concern. Theaters held benefit performances for those unfortunate people captured by the pirates. Susanna Rowson wrote a play on the topic, *Slaves in Algiers* (1794). A number of books about Algeria were published, some of which Tyler may have consulted.[3] Tyler's interest in Algeria and in captivity was also a personal matter. A Tyler descendant explains, ". . . in the family tradition . . .'The Algerian Captive' was our first ancestor, Thomas Tyler, a sea captain. . . . His last voyage was in 1703, when he was taken by a Barbary corsair . . . carried into Algiers, and has never been heard of since. . . ."[4]

In addition, Royall Tyler might have been influenced in choosing his topic by the great popularity of captivity narratives, stories about prisoners of the Indians.[5] Tyler had personally known one of these prisoners. When Tyler first brought his bride to Vermont, they visited "Mrs. Tute, celebrated as 'The Fair Captive,' " who had once been taken prisoner "by a party of hostile Indians."[6] Thus, Tyler's novel combined public and personal interests.

The Algerine Captive was one of the first American novels to be reprinted in London (G. & J. Robinson, 1802, 2 volumes). A warehouse fire destroyed nearly all of these copies, however, and the novel was then reprinted in the *Lady's Magazine* of London (1804). A second American edition (in one volume) was published in Hartford, Connecticut, by Peter B. Gleason in 1816. Parts of the book also appeared in the *Farmer's Weekly Museum*—Part I, Chapter 18 (the early adventures of a physician), on August 14, 1797; and Part II, Chapter 14 (concerning the Moslem faith), on August 21, 1797. *The Algerine Captive* is the second American novel about American life. It was preceded and possibly influenced by Hugh Henry Brackenridge's *Modern Chivalry* (1792, 1793, 1797, 1815). Tyler's is the first novel about life in New England.[7]

To offset the Puritan-inspired prejudice against fiction, eighteenth-century novels frequently claimed to be true stories.[8] In this tradition, *The Algerine Captive* (using a quotation from Shakespeare's *Othello)* purports to be "a round unvarnished tale. . . ."[9] The book is dedicated to David Humphreys, a playwright, political figure, and Connecticut wit. The dedication praises Humphreys' work in helping to settle the American conflict with the Algerians.[10]

The novel's preface is an early assertion of the need for Americans to create their own manners and their own literature. This statement echoes the comments about "homespun arts" which had been stated earlier in the prologue to *The Contrast*. The preface of *The Algerine Captive*, like the entire novel, is supposedly written by the first-person narrator, Updike Underhill. After Underhill's return from Algeria, he observes and deplores the popularity of "books designed to amuse rather than to instruct. . ." (p. 27).

Underhill objects to the fact that so many popular books ". . . are not of our own manufacture. . . ." He also notes that the English novel ". . . excites a fondness for false splendor" and makes the "homespun habits" of America seem "disgusting" (p. 28). Updike recommends ". . . that we write our own books of amusement and that they exhibit our own manners" (p. 28). Both purposes are achieved in the first volume of *The Algerine Captive*.

II The Algerine Captive, *Volume I*

In Volume I of *The Algerine Captive*, the satire is for the most part good natured. The youthful hero and narrator of the novel, Updike Underhill, has been described as a "yankee Candide."[11] Certainly Updike is a young man with vast illusions about life. As he proceeds through the painful process of growing up, of initiation into reality, Updike learns that the world is not perfect.

The opening chapters of *The Algerine Captive* deal with Updike's ancestor Captain John Underhill, an actual person who came to America in about 1630.[12] These three chapters "are historically *correct* according to the Underhill records. . . ."[13] After various adventures, Captain John Underhill emigrated to Massachusetts, from which he was eventually banished for what is described as "ADULTERY OF THE HEART. . ." (p. 36). Captain Underhill's descendant, Updike, was born on July 16, 1762.

As is customary for his time, young Updike attends a summer school taught by a woman and a winter school taught by a man. At age twelve, Updike impresses the local minister when "I recited as loud as I could speak . . ." (p. 45). For four years Updike studies with the minister. He learns Greek and Latin but not English, for "my preceptor knowing nothing of it himself, could communicate nothing to me" (p. 46). After Updike's father suffers a financial reverse, the young man must go back to the farm. There Updike tries to apply his classical learning, ". . . but, alas, a taste for Greek had quite eradicated a love for labor" (p. 50).

Finally Updike tries an experiment based on Virgil's *Georgics*. To raise a swarm of bees, he slaughters a cow and allows it to putrefy. The experiment fails, ". . . and my father consented . . . that I should renew my career of learning" (p. 50). This kind of naive understatement is part of the humor in Volume I.

To raise money, Updike becomes a schoolmaster. Again illusion conflicts with reality. The young man daydreams about ". . . my scholars, seated in awful silence around me. . ." (p. 51). Updike anticipates independence with his salary. He looks forward to finding "amusement and pleasure" among the young people and "information and delight" in conversations with the minister (p. 52).

The time comes to test these youthful hopes. Sixty scholars gather; study is impossible because of the "incessant clamor" (p. 52). Other illusions are quickly destroyed. The young people of the area neither understand nor appreciate Updike's references to classical literature.[14] Despite Updike's arguments, the town's minister remains convinced that the English version of the Psalms "is the same in language, letter, and metre, with those Psalms King David chanted in the city of Jerusalem" (p. 54).

Then Updike is told that he will not receive his wages until the spring. The wages will be in produce which he himself must harvest. Thoroughly disillusioned, Updike is relieved when the school burns down. He reflects, ". . . my emancipation from real slavery in Algiers did not afford me sincerer joy than I experienced at that moment" (p. 55).

Now Updike decides to study with a physician. Updike tells about the blind Dr. Moyes, a popular lecturer on optics. (The real Henry Moyes and Tyler had both roomed with the Palmer family in the late 1780s. Tyler "used to assist him [Moyes]at his public lectures."[15])

Updike's quotations from the classics are still unappreciated and misunderstood. His attempt to compliment a young lady in poetry provokes her jealous suitor to protest: "Them there very extraordinary pare of varses . . . . I shall be happy to do myself the onner of wasting a few charges of powder with you. . ." (p. 67). Updike is puzzled by what he thinks is "an invitation to shoot partridges. . ." (p. 68). Informed that he has been challenged to a duel, Updike comments, ". . . the principal difference between a man of honor and a vulgar murderer is that . . . the former will write you complaisant letters, and smile in your face, and bow gracefully, while he cuts your throat" (p. 69).

Learning that Updike has calmly accepted the challenge, his opponent is terrified and informs the authorities. Updike is arrested "by the high sheriff, two deputies, three constables, and eleven stout assistants, and carried in the dead of the night before the magistrates, where I met my antagonist, guarded by a platoon of the militia. . ." (p. 70). (Exaggeration or hyperbole is a staple of American comic fiction.) The two young men are forced to shake hands. Updike comments sarcastically on the effect of the duel: ". . . if I had spouted a whole *Iliad* in the ballroom, no one would have ventured to interrupt me; for I had proved myself a MAN OF HONOR" (p. 71).

His medical training completed, Updike visits the college museum at Harvard. "Here, to my surprise, I found the curiosities of all countries but our own" (p. 78). *The Algerine Captive* stresses the need for Americans to learn about themselves.

Updike starts practicing his profession in a town where there already are four physicians: "The learned doctor," "The cheap doctor," "The safe doctor," and a fourth who has the largest practice, for he is an entertaining person and "well gifted in prayer" (p. 82). Medical quackery is one of Tyler's pet peeves.[16]

Still seeking a place to practice medicine, Updike goes to the South. There his illusions are again destroyed. At church on Sunday, a young minister fiercely beats his slave, then preaches "an animated discourse" on the commandment "Remember the Sabbath day. . ." (p. 94). The minister next rushes to a horse race, where he acts as turf judge. Not only is the South a disappointment to Updike, but he is a disappointment to the southerners: "The very decorum, prudence, and economy which would have enhanced my character at home were here construed into poverty of spirit" (p. 97).

Eventually Updike accepts a berth as a surgeon on a ship bound for Africa. The ship stops in England, where it is sold. Updike describes the British in strong terms: "A motley race in whose mongrel veins runs the blood of all nations; . . . languishing wretched lives in fetid jails; and boasting of the GLORIOUS FREEDOM OF ENGLISHMEN" (p. 99). (Similar comments appear in Tyler's *Yankey in London,* 1809.) In London, Updike meets Thomas Paine, whose "bodily presence was both mean and contemptible" (p. 102). Several uncomplimentary anecdotes about Paine follow. Some of Tyler's essays and poems also criticize Paine.

Updike leaves England in July 1788 and sails for Africa aboard a slave ship, ironically named *Sympathy* (p. 107). Updike is appalled to hear the traders ". . . converse upon the purchase of human beings with the same indifference . . . as if they were contracting for so many head of cattle. . ." (p. 108). Updike's sensibility is affected. He imagines ". . . the fond husband torn from the embraces of his beloved wife; the mother, from her babes; the tender child, from the arms of its parent. . ." (p. 108). The young man chides himself for "even the involuntary part I bore in this execrable traffic" (p. 109).

Updike prays ". . . that the miseries, the insults, and cruel woundings I afterwards received when a slave myself may expiate for the inhumanity I was necessitated to exercise towards these, MY BRETHREN OF THE HUMAN RACE" (p. 110). The chapters about slavery are not satire; they reveal Tyler's repugnance for this institution.

Chapter 31 depicts the condition of the slaves on the ship and the "heart-rending bursts of sorrow and despair" (p. 112). When the slaves begin to sicken and die, the weakest are landed on the coast under Updike's care. On November 14, 1788, Updike's ship is chased away by a strange vessel, stranding the physician on the shore. Four days later Algerian pirates capture Updike.

At this point, Volume I of *The Algerine Captive* ends. When William Dunlap read the book in 1797, he began "with great pleasure" which decreased when Updike sailed abroad.[17] The satire of Volume I is more lighthearted than the attacks upon slavery and the ponderous descriptions in Volume II.

III The Algerine Captive, *Volume II*

For many years, the Barbary Coast pirates had preyed upon European shipping. After the Revolutionary War, the United States was no longer protected by English naval power. As early as 1779 the Continental Congress had attempted with no success to make treaties with the pirate states. The young nation began paying tribute and preparing for the inevitable military solution.[18] Fully aware of the great interest in the pirates and their prisoners, Royall Tyler tried to make Volume II of *The Algerine Captive* more than an adventure story. He combined a travelogue with a captivity narrative.

Taken into Algiers, Updike is exhibited for sale. His experience parallels the humiliating treatment of African slaves by Americans, a treatment which had earlier aroused Updike's indignation. During Updike's captivity, many of his illusions are destroyed: "I did not meet, among my fellow slaves, the rich and noble, as the dramatist and the novelist had taught me to expect" (p. 126). When Updike is struck by an overseer, the young American knocks down his tormentor. As punishment, Updike is sent to work in the stone quarries.[19]

Attempts are made to convert Updike to his captors' religion. He resists: "I had ever viewed the character of an apostate as odious and detestable. . . . My body is in slavery, but my mind is free. . ." (p. 134). The weary Updike finally agrees to speak with the Moslem priest, the Mollah, partly to be relieved of his heavy labor and partly from curiosity. The Mollah is a former Christian, learned in Latin and in Christian doctrine. Updike had been prepared for "force and terror. . . ." At the Mollah's gentle treatment, Updike "trembled for my faith and burst into tears" (p. 138).

In Chapter 7, Updike and the Mollah converse at length about the comparative values of the Christian and Moslem religions. Updike is disconcerted when the Mollah refers to slavery in America, where the Americans "baptize the unfortunate African into your faith, and then use your brother Christians as brutes of the desert" (p. 142). After five days of discussion, Updike is ". . . almost confounded by his sophistry . . ." and seeks "safety in my former servitude" (p. 143).

After the interlude with the Mollah, Updike's return to the quarries is even more "insupportable" (p. 146). He plans to escape but changes his mind after seeing the "fiend-like punishment" of a slave who had attempted to get away (p. 149). Now Updike feels that he is truly a slave. He is anxious to "conciliate" the overseer. Only as a slave has he "learned to appreciate the blessings of freedom" (p. 151).

Falling ill, Updike is sent to an infirmary in the city of Algiers. There he is visited by the Mollah, who persuades the director of the infirmary to purchase Updike. The American comments, "If any man could have effected a change of my religion, it was this priest" (p. 153). Updike is allowed to practice as a physician in Algiers. He meets with "arrant bunglers," "professional ignorance and obstinacy," and "religious prejudice" (pp. 154 - 55).

In Chapters 15 to 28, plot and characterization are suspended while Updike describes Algerian history, geography, religion, government, law, customs, and so on. In Chapter 29, Updike returns to center stage. One day he is approached by an elderly Jew, Adonah Ben Benjamin, whose son is ill.[20] (The son's name is never given.) Updike cures the son and wins the father as a friend. Adonah promises to help the captive save up his money in order to pay his own ransom. Unfortunately, two days before the boat for freedom is to leave, Adonah suddenly dies. The son is as treacherous as the father was trustworthy. When Adonah's son denies knowing about the money Updike had banked, the betrayed American becomes dejected. Travel is recommended to restore him. Chapters 31 to 34 describe Updike's visits to Medina and Mecca.

Among the group of travelers is Adonah's wicked son, who again becomes ill. He begs the physician for help. In return, the son promises to assist Updike to escape. Once cured, Adonah's son arranges passage for Updike aboard a ship headed for Gibraltar. But the treacherous young man has actually sold Updike into slavery again, and to an extremely cruel master (pp. 219 - 22).

Fortunately for Updike, the ship is damaged by a storm and overtaken by a Portuguese frigate. Updike is at last released from slavery. He sails to Portugal, then returns home in May 1795,

". . . after an absence of seven years and one month, about six years of which I had been a slave" (p. 224). The young man sentimentally recalls his situation and his emotions: "I had suffered hunger, sickness, fatigue, insult, stripes, wounds, and every other cruel injury. . . . I had been degraded to a slave, and was now advanced to a citizen of the freest country in the universe" (p. 224).

Updike plans to get married, to continue his medical practice, ". . . and to contribute cheerfully to the support of our excellent government, which I have learnt to adore in schools of despotism." He hopes that from his experiences his fellow citizens can learn ". . . the necessity of uniting our federal strength. . . ." A Federalist effusion concludes the novel: "For to no nation besides the United States can that ancient saying be more emphatically applied; BY UNITING WE STAND, BY DIVIDING WE FALL" (p. 224).[21]

IV *Commentary*

In depicting the comically named Updike Underhill, Tyler portrays an American innocent.[22] Although Updike confuses reality and illusion, he does not become cynical as he learns about the real world.[23] In New England he responds with humor at realizing the absence of the perfection about which he dreams. In the South and especially on the slave ship, Updike expresses moral indignation. In Algeria, Updike learns to value his own liberty. Like a sentimental hero, Updike is benevolent and uncorrupted by the evil he encounters.

Updike is a persona or mask for the author; the young man is a character through whom the story is told. Tyler uses Updike as his spokesman on a variety of topics, especially for his opinions about slavery. As a judge, Tyler strongly opposed slavery. In one law case Tyler was asked what would be "sufficient evidence" of the ownership of an escaped slave. The judge replied, "A quit claim deed of ownership from the *Almighty*."[24] In another case, Tyler wrote a decision affirming that ". . . no inhabitant of the State [Vermont] can hold a slave. . . ."[25] In *The Algerine Captive* Tyler implies some parallels between the slavery of blacks in the United States and the experiences of the young American in Algiers.

Allied to the statements opposing slavery are numerous comments about the United States. In Volume I despite Updike's many disillusionments, he never loses his patriotism. In Volume II this devotion becomes even stronger. The novel is not only patriotic; it is also political. *The Algerine Captive*, especially in its conclusion, expresses support for a strong and unified central government. In Tyler's novel, out of adversity come federalist politics.

In addition, the novel contains several statements about the need for religious toleration. The tolerant descriptions of Mahometanism resulted in Tyler's being accused of appearing to favor the Moslem.[26] Tyler denied this charge. (See below, Section V.)

The novel reveals the diversified knowledge and wide reading of its author. Besides the many interesting details about life in early New England, conditions in England and Algeria are described. In the narrator's words, ". . . the best European authorities" have been used for information.[27]

The novel abounds in literary references. For example, in less than three pages, the preface refers to broadside reports of speeches by dying criminals, Michael Wigglesworth's poem "The Day of Doom," John Bunyan's *Pilgrim's Progress*, travel books by Patrick Brydone and James Bruce, the Gothic novels of Ann Radcliffe, the essays of Joseph Addison, and the *Parallel Lives* of Plutarch (pp. 27 - 29).

Each of the sixty-nine chapters begins with a quotation from some source. These quotations are an indication of Tyler's reading and of the reading done by educated people in New England in the late 1790s. Among the sources quoted are Shakespeare (9 times), Alexander Pope (7), Edward Young (5), William Cowper (3), Samuel "Hudibras" Butler (3), Horace (2), Milton (2), and the Bible (2). There are single quotations from Jonathan Edwards, Ethan Allen, James Thomson's "Seasons," Robert Blair, Mark Akenside, Oliver Goldsmith, Laurence Sterne, Edward Coke, Rabelais, Lilly, Virgil, and others. In addition, thirteen of the headnotes are original to Tyler, described as being from the "AUTHOR'S *Manuscript Poems*." (See Chapter 7 for a discussion of some of these headnotes.)

Besides the headnotes, numerous classical references can be found—particularly to Virgil and Homer. Tyler also demonstrates his familiarity with the writings of John Locke, Thomas Paine, and with various works on religion, law, and medicine. He makes specific use of or refers to a number of literary works, including satires by Peter Pindar and romantic stories about idealized slaves by Mrs. Aphra Behn and George Colman, the younger. Tyler's wide reading and keen intellect are amply illustrated in *The Algerine Captive*.

V *Reactions to the Novel*

Although most readers liked *The Algerine Captive,* the novel's sales were not large. Aaron Burr's law partner, William Coleman, wrote, "I have heard . . . applause for your literary talents . . . the 'public curiosity is said to be alive to read [*The Algerine Captive*]. . . .' "[28] In a letter dated August 30, 1797, Tyler's friend Joseph Dennie commented, "Your novel has been examined by the few and approved." Dennie also warned, "It is however extremely difficult for the Bostonians to supply themselves with a book that slumbers in a stall at Walpole. . . ."[29] One English review of 1803 said that the reader is ". . . . carried along by a train of probable and touching events; . . . [and is] pleased with natural and lively painting. . . ."[30]

In 1810, a "Retrospective Review" appeared in the *Monthly Anthology and Boston Review.* The reviewer says of *The Algerine Captive,* "This little work is very undeservedly hastening to oblivion. It contains an admirable picture of the manners of the interior of New England. . . ." The reviewer also takes issue with Tyler's "perpetual invective against classical learning. . . ." Like most critics, the anonymous reviewer finds the second volume "much inferiour to the first." The reviewer continues, "There is one chapter, however . . . which deserves the most pointed reprehension. It is the conversation between Updike and the Mollah [the Moslem priest]. . . . The author has so decidedly given the Mollah the best of the argument, that the adherence of Updike to Christianity seems the effect rather of obstinacy than of conviction. We enter our solemn protest against this cowardly mode of attacking revelation."[31]

Tyler's answer to these charges was written some time after 1820: "The Author . . . never imagined it [the novel] was objectionable on the score of infidelity or even scepticism. The part objected to . . . was written with a view to do away the vulgar prejudices against [Islam]. He never thought that . . . he was even jeopardizing the truths of Christianity, for . . . the Mahometan imposture will be obvious to those who compare . . . the monstrous absurdities of the Koran, with the sublime doctrines, morals & language of the Gospel dispensation."[32] Such was Tyler's defense.

In 1822 James Fenimore Cooper wrote about books which "illustrate American society and manners. . . ." He favorably mentioned a book entitled *Salem Witchcraft* and "Mr. Tyler's forgotten, and we fear, lost narrative of the Algerine Captive. . . . Any future collector of our national tales, would do well to snatch these from oblivion, and to give them that place among the memorials of other days, which is due to the early and authentic historians of a country."[33]

Modern commentators have also been generous. Arthur Hobson Quinn says that Tyler's satiric fiction ". . . has at times an imaginative quality."[34] Carl Van Doren writes, "The value of the book lies largely in its report of facts, which it gives clearly and freshly."[35] Alexander Cowie comments, ". . . light satire patently was his [Tyler's] forte, and his crisp, classic prose was ideally suited to be its vehicle." Calling Tyler "superior to the average popular novelist," Cowie describes Tyler's language as "swift, well balanced, allusive but comparatively unembellished—which lends interest to his satire. . . ."[36] Frank Chandler describes Updike as a picaresque figure, "a good humored, matter-of-fact satirist, pricking the bubbles of life. . . ."[37]

VI The Bay Boy

On November 13, 1824, Mary Palmer Tyler recorded in her diary, "This day My Husband wrote the first slate full of the New Edition of the Algerine C—"[38] The difficulties must have been enormous. The Tyler family was in desperate financial condition. The author's eyesight was so poor that he could no longer write easily on paper. He would make the revisions in large letters on a slate. His wife would then transcribe these notes for her husband.

The painfully ill Tyler was able to do what he rarely had done before—he revised and improved upon his writing. What Tyler achieved in *The Bay Boy* gives no indication of the conditions under which the book was written. The new work is delightful, filled with humor and vivid local color. The following analysis will show the basic differences between the original novel and its revision:[39]

The Algerine Captive	*The Bay Boy*
Chs. 1 - 3, Capt. John Underhill	omitted
Ch. 4, Updike's birth	omitted
	Ch. I, Updike's mother (new material)
	Ch. II, Updike's birth (new material)

Ch. 5, Updike's schooling	Ch. III, Updike's schooling (revised)
	Ch. IV, Updike's teacher, Reverend Priest (new material)
	Ch. V, The Town of Shingletrees (new material)
Ch. 6, Updike's father discusses Classical Education with a visitor	Ch. VI, Updike's studies (including parts of Chs. 5 and 6 of *Captive)*
Chs. 7 - 8, Updike teaches school; his social life; he chooses a vocation—medicine	Ch. VII, Updike teaches school; his social life; he chooses a vocation (incorporates Chs. 7 and 8 of *Captive)*
	Ch. VIII, Updike's first love; he goes to Harvard (both sections are new material)
	Ch. IX, "Sunday in Boston in the year 17—." Updike studies medicine: Sunday in Boston; introducing Mrs. Diaway (all sections are new material)
	Ch.X, At Mrs. Diaway's house; Miss Charlotte Love; the warden (all sections are new material)
Chs. 9 - 11, Operation on a blind man; Doctor Moyes; Updike and Greek	Ch. XI, Blindness and its cure; Dr. Moyes; social life (incorporates Chs. 9 - 11 of *Captive)*
	Ch. XII, "First Theatrical Representation in Boston" (new material)
	Ch. XIII, Updike writes a poem (new material)
	Ch. XIV, " 'Jealousy.' " Updike on Shakespeare; Mrs. Diaway and Charlotte Love; treatment of blacks in Boston (all sections are new material)
	Ch. XV, "Thanksgiving and Christmas Days." In Boston; the party (both sections are new material)

The individual chapters in *The Bay Boy* are generally longer and more detailed than the chapters in *The Algerine Captive*. Possibly at the suggestion of Tyler's son Edward, the long introductory summaries before each chapter of *The Algerine Captive* have been omitted.[40]

The subtitle of the revision indicates Tyler's intentions: ". . . to preserve some traces of those evanescent customs, habits, manners, opinions and notions which prevailed among the good people of Boston & its vicinity during a period anterior to the Revolution / by a native of Boston" (p. 41). There are three prefaces. The "Preface to the Second Edition" explains that *The Algerine Captive* was written by Tyler "at the suggestion of his lamented friend, the late Joseph Dennie. . ." (pp. 45 - 46). Tyler comments that the London edition of *Captive* was well treated by reviewers despite the statement that " 'no one ever read an American book' " (p. 46). Sidney Smith made his famous statement in 1820: "In the four quarters of the globe, who reads an American book. . . ?"[41] Thus, Tyler's "Preface to the Second Edition" was written in or after 1820.

The Bay Boy begins with a description of Updike's mother, Molly. The daughter of Ichabod Anvil, a Boston hardware merchant, Molly ". . . was taught every accomplishment. . . . She cut paper. . . . She painted on glass. . ." (p. 50). Molly's "literary acquirements" are also described. She read the Bible, the *New-England Primer,* Richardson's sentimental novel *Pamela,* Anne Bradstreet's poems, "and would have read Young's Night Thoughts, only as she said it puzzled her so to make out the rhymes" (p. 53; Young's poem, being in blank verse, has no rhymes). Molly's main achievement was playing the spinet.

Unfortunately, Molly was not accomplished in the practical arts. In spelling ". . . she uniformly substituted the P for the B and vice versa. . . ." Updike reprints Molly's "Resate to macka Boun kake . . ." (p. 55). This is an early example of cacography (incorrect spelling), which is a frequent source of humor in American writing.

In spite of Molly's accomplishments, she remained unmarried. Eventually, she met "a hale bachelor of forty. . ." (p. 56). When Molly casually mentioned that she was in possession of an independent income of £3,000 and would inherit more money, she won her husband. And she proved her worth. Updike explains that Molly's ". . . town education was imparted by fashion, . . . [but] her conjugal duties and matronly graces were taught by those sage instructors—reason, experience and good sense" (p. 57). Molly became "an excellent housewife. . ." (p. 58).

In Chapter II of *The Bay Boy* Updike says that he was born in Shingletrees, near Boston, on February 22, but conceals the exact year. He hopes to prevent a future reviewer from arguing that the book's descriptions are inaccurate. Later chapters contain references which suggest that *The Bay Boy* is set in the 1760s and 1770s, the years when Tyler himself was growing toward manhood.[42]

In Chapter III (as in Chapter 5 of *The Algerine Captive*), Updike attracts attention with his stentorian voice. Molly proclaims, "Updike shall have learning. . . . He certainly has two most striking marks of a great genius about him: he hates work and loves books" (p. 63). Updike is sent to study with the Reverend Ammi Rhuhamah Priest, who is described in Chapter IV. The second half of Chapter IV is rich in local color. Updike describes sowing, cutting wood for fuel, and the annual slaughter for meat. Chapter V contains a story about the building of a road. This allegory illustrates Tyler's advocacy of religious toleration.

Chapter VI of *The Bay Boy* includes part of Chapter 5 and all of Chapter 6 from *The Algerine Captive*. Chapter VII of *The Bay Boy* combines Chapters 7 and 8 of *The Algerine Captive*. Chapter VIII of *The Bay Boy* is a delightful addition. At church the seventeen-year-old Updike is overwhelmed by a "beautiful cherry cheeked girl. . ." (p. 95). His mother cleverly arranges for Updike to pay an unannounced social call on the young lady. Entering her kitchen, Updike sees the "divine charmer" dressed in dirty clothing and laboring over a vat of raw wool (p. 98). The girl's conversation is no more attractive than her appearance. "The charm of *first love* was broken" (p. 98).

Shortly after this disillusioning experience, Updike enters Harvard. Unfortunately, no details about his experiences there are given. After graduating from Harvard, Updike becomes (in Chapter IX) a student of Dr. G., a Boston physician.[43]

Chapter IX contains a vivid description of "Sunday in Boston in the Year 17—" (p. 101). On Saturday evening, ". . . the old South clock struck eight and all was silence" (p. 103).[44] The description of a Puritan Sunday in Boston is fascinating: ". . . not a person appeared to interrupt the solemn stillness of the streets" (pp. 103 - 104). Updike describes the morning church service, the dinner of "plum pudding and roast beef" (p. 107), and the afternoon service where he and a number of other worshipers are "refreshed by an excellent sermon and . . . by a comfortable nap" (p. 108).

When Updike returns home, he finds Doctor G. preparing medicine for a patient. Mrs. Diaway, the doctor explains, is a childless widow with a large estate and nothing to do. Like many gentlewomen of her times, including Molly Anvil, Mrs. Diaway is a victim of the miseducation of women. The widow has become a hypochondriac. Updike is sent to deliver some harmless pills to the patient.

The deserted Sabbath streets remind Updike of a "petrified city" (p. 113). An occasional sound comes from the houses, usually of someone reading from a religious book. The only activity to be seen involves some boys, including a young black named Pompey, who are fishing from a window with a string and bent pin.[45]

In Chapter X the warden stops Updike. Updike later describes a warden: ". . . there was irresistable authority in the very creak of his shoe leather!" (p. 130). The fledgling physician explains his mission and is permitted to proceed after being advised "to avoid these errands as far as practicable on the Lord's day . . . and to avoid too critical a survey of the contents of the windows and signposts" (p. 118).

Updike reaches the home of Mrs. Diaway, which he describes in some detail, providing insights into the customs and furnishings of the time. Next Updike meets Mrs. Diaway's beautiful niece, Miss Charlotte Love (p. 125). The young man tries to compliment Charlotte, who is not favorably impressed by his attentions.

Chapter XI of *The Bay Boy* is a composite of Chapters 9, 10, and 11 of *The Algerine Captive.* Chapter XII of *The Bay Boy* contains original material describing the "First Theatrical Representation in Boston" (p. 141). Updike is invited, "under the strongest injunctions of secrecy" (p. 142), to attend a surreptitious performance of Joseph Addison's *Cato* (1713). Updike approves, since the play has ". . . many fine passages about liberty. . ." (p. 143). The arrival of the constables puts an end to the performance, but most of the cast escapes, as does Updike. Such clandestine productions might have helped to develop Tyler's understanding of theater and of dramatic techniques.

Chapter XIII returns to the intriguing relationship between Updike and Charlotte Love. At a tea party the pretty and spirited girl had given a mocking description of the apprentice physician. In revenge Updike writes for the *Massachusetts Spy* a poem entitled "The Wolf and Wooden Beauty." (This poem by Tyler originally appeared in the magazine *Polyanthos,* May 1807.[46]) In *The Bay Boy,* lines 13 and 14 are altered slightly to add the name of the girl being satirized. The poem warns men not to be deceived by outward appearances, and laments, "But what is beauty without brains?" (p. 152). Charlotte seems to take no notice of the poem, and the two young people become increasingly friendly. They read together from Samuel Richardson's sentimental novel of romance *Sir Charles Grandison* (1753 - 54; also read by Maria in *The Contrast*).

Updike becomes a great favorite with Mrs. Diaway's servants

when he rescues the widow's black servant Zack from a mob of white men. Apparently, in pre-Revolutionary Boston, it was the custom on Commencement Day at Harvard to duck blacks in the river. Updike decides that this was "one of the few bad customs which was purely colonial" (p. 162).

Chapter XV, the last extant chapter from *The Bay Boy*, is entitled "Thanksgiving and Christmas Days" (p. 164). It contains some valuable descriptions of pre-Revolutionary manners, customs, and foods. Updike goes to his Grandmother Anvil's house for Thanksgiving. He describes the banquet in detail. After the dinner, fruits, nuts, and wines are served. One of the toasts asks for "Prosperity to the American provinces—united we stand, divided we fall" (p. 167).[47]

Christmas Eve at Dr. G's home is also described, beginning with the entry into the house of a group of mummers: ". . . grotesquely dressed, their faces masked, several of them armed with wooden swords and daggers, . . . [the mummers] immediately began to enact a little farce or comedy" (p. 168). On Christmas Day, Updike attends church and returns for dinner to Dr. G's home. "The feast rivaled Thanksgiving in plenty and sumptuousness. . ." (p. 169). Political differences are revealed in the toasts at the home of Dr. G, who is a Tory. Toasting the king and the entire royal family, the celebrants wish "confusion to those who would bring confusion into the colonies" (p. 169). As a Whig, Updike drinks his toasts "with mental reservation" (p. 170). He says that the Loyalists at the Christmas dinner "lived to discern that they were false prophets . . ." (p. 170).

On Twelfth Night, the doctor sponsors a ball. Updike dances happily with Charlotte and introduces her to his friend Charles Brightly. After Brightly escorts the girl to the supper table, the unhappy Updike is told by his own supper partner that there is a mystery connected with Charlotte's background and name. Updike sees Charlotte home, but she speaks admiringly of Charles. The young physician is too naive to realize that Charlotte's earlier adverse description of him "augured more in my favor than all her commendation did in favor of Charles Brightly" (p. 174). Then Updike repeats his supper partner's words, "I say nothing." With this ironic statement, *The Bay Boy* concludes.

The book contains brilliant descriptions of life in the country, of rural schools, a surgeon's practice in Boston, a silent Sunday in the Puritan-dominated city, a clandestine theatrical production, a mummers' play, and holiday foods and customs. These descriptions make the novel a valuable source of information about pre-Revolutionary New England.

Updike Underhill is a clever, perceptive, and often amusing narrator. He is different from the Updike of *The Algerine Captive*. The first novel is written from the point of view of the captive shortly after his return. The second novel is written from the point of view of an old man looking back on his early years. In the opening sections of *The Bay Boy*, Updike's youthful naiveté adds depth and irony to the story. The narrator is occasionally nostalgic, recalling details of an earlier way of life. He is not a detached wanderer; he is closely aware of life and of people. In *The Bay Boy*, both Tyler and his persona have mellowed. Both are closer to the daily life around them, less remote, less satirical.

Among the new characters, Charlotte Love is a sprightly and attractive young lady. The romance and the implied mystery about Charlotte pique the reader's interest. Tyler's depiction of the lonely hypochondriac Mrs. Diaway reveals a genuine understanding of human nature. *The Bay Boy* has much to recommend it, especially its characterization and its wealth of local-color descriptions.

But Royall Tyler was dying. He could not finish the book. On January 19, 1825, Mary wrote to her daughter Amelia about the revision: ". . . it is now laid by for the present——your Father's health is weak—and he got tired of the Captive—and wanted some recreation—and has been writing ever since I wrote you last, Several little Dramas. . . ."[48]

Unfortunately, *The Bay Boy* was never completed. But in it Tyler accomplished a considerable literary feat. One commentator notes of Tyler, ". . . in his last days, under the painful and melancholy inroads of a cancer, scintillations from his happy genius would occasionally burst forth."[49] *The Bay Boy* is one such scintillation.

CHAPTER 5

The Satirical Yankey

IN 1808, Royall Tyler was in correspondence with the New York publisher Isaac Riley about a collection of Vermont law reports.[1] The law reports were published in 1809 and 1810.[2] In October 1809 Riley also published Tyler's collection of fictional letters from an American traveler, *The Yankey in London*.[3]

I *The History of* Yankey

On June 10, 1809, Tyler sent Riley the manuscript of *The Yankey in London:* "The copy sent will, I am sensible, make but a small book; but from the preface, you will learn it may be enlarged." Tyler received $200 from Riley for the copyright.[4] Attempting to conceal his authorship, the judge wrote, "The remainder of the letters are not in Vermont, but can be commanded."[5] On October 7, 1809, Riley sent Tyler ". . . a copy of 'The Yanke in London' hastily put up. Some, more handsomely bound, I shall forward soon. . . . I have to ask you to aid me in procuring the future Letters to make a more enlarged edition."[6] Tyler acknowledged the copy: "I am exceedingly pleased with the elegant impression of the Yankee, but can say nothing as to another edition until the beginning of July. . . ."[7] There is no further correspondence about a subsequent edition, and no second volume was issued.

Like Volume II of *The Algerine Captive, Yankey* demonstrates Tyler's ability to assimilate a large body of information and to present that information in a clear and interesting manner. Although Tyler had never visited England, many readers believed that the letters were authentic. For instance, a neighbor of the Tylers, the Reverend William Wells, commented, ". . . the young man has been there and seen and heard what he vouches for. . . ." Reverend Wells did eventually learn the truth "and had a hearty laugh . . . about it. . . ."[8]

II The Yankey in London

The book's short preface is signed by "The Friends of the Writer." The preface describes the author as "a native of Boston . . . a gentleman of an active and inquisitive mind, and of quaint, and ofttimes original remark" (p. iii). His letters were written "without the most distant view of their ever being printed" (p. iv). The preface creates a realistic atmosphere for the fictional letters which are to follow.

The book is 180 pages long, and consists of thirteen letters. In order to suggest that these are selected from a larger volume of correspondence, the letters are numbered in a non-consecutive manner, starting with number III and ending with number XLV. Except for Letter XXIII, all of the correspondence is addressed to the writer's friend, a young man named Frank. (See pp. 27, 48, *et passim.) The Yankey in London* is fiction, but it is not a novel. There is no continuity, no plot, and—except for the creation of the unnamed letter writer—little characterization. The book is a series of essay-like observations written in a clever, relaxed style which is at times reminiscent of Addison and Steele.

The first letter (numbered III) is entitled "Certain Prominent Traits in the English Character. . . ." The Yankey explains that he ". . . wished to see *Englishmen,* and to form some correct estimate of their manners, habits, and character. . ." (pp. 3 - 4). The writer goes on to make a balanced and witty comparison: ". . . the Englishman is shy and suspicious, grows more suspicious, and is surly. The New-England man is suspicious and inquisitive, grows more suspicious, and is familiar and troublesome" (p. 6).

The writer also explains how to gain admission to the "*blue-stocking club*" of Mrs. Montagu: ". . . hasten to your ink-pot, tag me a hundred lines to some languishing Anna Matilda, or dying Dorinda; spangle them well with bland metaphors and love-lorn similes; drop a word or two in some lines, and insert others in capital letters . . . or write a lugubrious sonnet to some captive mouse, or pretty pathetic ode to a sportive mouser . . ." (pp. 12 - 13). This description satirizes the Della Cruscan style of poetry, which Tyler parodied in such poems as "Address to Della Crusca" and "Sonnet to an Old Mouser."[9]

In the first letter, Tyler also satirizes the Gothic novel. He mentions a woman who "had published a novel which contained . . . two crazy castles; three murderers; a trap-door with rusty bolts; a bloody key, ditto dagger; . . . a sheeted ghost; a ghostly monk, and a marriage" (p. 15). The lady's prose contained such distinguished oxymorons as "pleasing anguish" and "delightful despair" (pp. 15 - 16).

The second letter (numbered V) is about the British House of Commons. There, the naive letter writer had expected to find "a solemn assembly of wise, dignified men, in sober consultation. . ." (p. 18). Instead, the first thing he hears is the placing of bets on a horse race.[10] The Yankey criticizes the members of the House of Commons for their coughing, whispering, talking, and laughing during speeches. To the Yankey, "a laughing legislature is . . . as incongruous as a skipping, tripping bishop. . ." (p. 27).[11] As is true throughout the book, behavior is described, not the physical appearance of the places supposedly visited.

The third letter (numbered VIII) contains a discussion of the House of Lords, which sits as "a high court of errors" (p. 35). The Yankey is amused at the idea of "*hereditary judges* . . ." (p. 35) and comments that in Parliament "the rights and interests of the landholders may be made subservient to the gains of the merchant and the rights, interests, and liberties of the common people sacrificed to both. . ." (p. 45).

The fourth letter (numbered XI) is entitled "English Biography." According to this letter, biographies should ". . . illustrate history, and present the most instructive lessons to mankind" (p. 48). But the object of English biographers is "to fill the vacuity of little minds. . ." (p. 50). The letter writer approves of ethical works which give the impression that ". . . the author lived an eminent example of the precepts he enjoined. . . ." The young Bostonian continues, ". . . you never had your heart warmed or your life amended by a sermon on temperance from a drunken parson" (p. 55). The Yankey objects to biographers such as James Boswell, who ". . . expose the infirmities of the wise for the gratification of the idle. . ." (p. 57). He castigates Samuel Johnson, who "set the fashion of this gossiping biography" in his *Lives of the Poets* (p. 58).

The fifth letter (numbered XIX) discusses two topics which are unexpectedly connected: "The London Booksellers—Etymology of the term Yankey" (p. 69). The writer describes the book shops of London and especially one bookseller from Yorkshire, where the natives are ". . . very subtle, if not dishonest" (p. 75). The letter writer explains jokingly, "The term Yankey is but a corruption of Yorkshire, being simply the Indian pronunciation" (p. 75).[12]

The sixth letter (numbered XX), "Strictures upon the decorous in public bodies," is a reply to a letter from the writer's friend Frank. Frank had apparently accused the writer of being too serious in his description of the House of Commons (Letter V). The Yankey (who sounds at times like Colonel Manly in *The Contrast)* insists that gravity is a "natural . . . attendant on wisdom . . ." (p. 77) and notes that "Washington and Adams were no jokers" (p. 79).

The seventh letter (numbered XXIII) is addressed to "My dear Sister" and is entitled "The sun—and fashion." The writer describes how even at noon the English sun "is obscured by clouds of sea-coal smoke. . ." (p. 86). This is one of the book's few specific descriptions of England. Then the writer goes on to discuss fashions: "The change of fashion, which with us is a whim, here is a principle: thousands get their bread by making ornamental dresses. . . ." If clothing were more durable, ". . . thousands would starve. . ." (p. 88). The letter continues in this satiric vein.

The eighth letter (numbered XXX) is headed "Bite—bamboozle—all the rage. . . ." It reveals an interest in language, especially in such "cant words, or quaint expressions" as "fellow," "clever," and "that's a good one" (p. 101). The Yankey disapproves of slang and fashionable phrases. He also makes an early comparison between American and British English: "An Englishman puts and answers a question directly, a New-Englandman puts his questions circuitously and always answers a question by asking another" (pp. 106 - 107).

The ninth letter in the book (numbered XXXIII) is the longest. It deals with "Literary larceny, forgery, and swindling. . . ." The letter discusses favorably the work of three literary forgers: Thomas Chatterton (1752 - 1770), William Henry Ireland (1777 - 1835), and James Macpherson (1736 - 1796).[13] The Yankey comments patriotically that Americans value books and men, ". . . not for their origin but their intrinsic merit. . ." (pp. 131 - 32). This statement may be naive or satirical, or it may be an expression of unrealized ideals. Tyler waged a continuing battle for the appreciation of American authors. (See the prologue to *The Contrast;* the preface to *The Algerine Captive;* Act I, Scene 1, of *The Island of Barrataria;* and the "Introduction to the Sacred Dramas.")

The book's tenth letter (numbered XLII) deals satirically with "Medical, mechanical, and culinary quacks." The letter writer claims that in England ". . . the belief in panaceas is a national weakness" (p. 134). Some comic examples are given of mechanical quackery, such as a testimonial distributed by a manufacturer of artificial eyes. In addition, the Yankey discusses a book which combines advice on culinary matters with "all the eminent nostrums and quack medicines of the day. . ." (p. 141). This book has chapters on "Apple-pye and Asthma," "Ragouts and Rheumatism," and "Fricasees and Fevers" (p. 142).

The eleventh letter (numbered XLIII) is entitled "Prominent traits in the English Character." First, there is vanity: "The English verily believe they are the most enlightened people in the world; the greatest in arts and arms; the uprightest, the wealthiest, the wisest . . . the *freest* people. . . !" (pp. 149 - 50). The writer sets out to refute these claims in a lengthy and not always moderate polemic.

The Yankey attacks ". . . the gas which inflates the full-blown bladder of English vanity"; that is, the English government, which has one great object, "the commercial aggrandizement of the nation . . ." (p. 154). The writer ends by claiming that he has been joking: ". . . if I could in a serious mood asperse a great people in this manner, I should abhor myself, and feel degraded from the rank of intelligent beings, and reduced to a level with *English travellers*" (p. 165). Satire is again evident in this statement.

The shortest letter in the book is the twelfth (numbered XLIV). Only four pages long, it is entitled "Introduction to the adventures of a young Bostonian, who went to London to establish *a credit.*" The letter describes an American dandy in England, ". . . dressed in the pink of the mode—his pockets full of cash, and his mouth full of wonder" (p. 168). He has seen the Monument, is going to have his picture painted, and plans a flirtation with a young lady. The fop is in contrast to the serious letter writer who has been to Parliament, has talked with a number of Englishmen, and has observed the people and manners of his host country.

The thirteenth and last letter (numbered XLV) is entitled "Strictures on the English language of the present day." Frank has asked the Yankey to compare English with the European languages. The Yankey replies, "I consider the Latin tongue in the Augustan Age, and the Greek in all the elder ages, to have been the noblest languages. . ." (pp. 172 - 73). Of all the modern languages, he prefers English because it is closer to ". . . the precious metals of the Greeks and Romans" (p. 174).

Then the letter discusses language as a dynamic force: "Language . . . partakes of the laws of our nature: it is ever changing. . . ." Modern English "already betrays the garrulity and weakness of old age;—it delights in gorgeous metaphors, in similes which sparkle but do not illustrate, and all the pretty prettinesses of verse-like prose" (p. 175). The Yankey complains, "I ask for elegant wit, and they hand me Peter Pindar—I inquire for sublimity, and they present me Della Crusca" (p. 179).

A postscript to the last letter refers once again to the financial misadventures of the young dandy who was described earlier. The book ends on this abrupt note.

III *Comments*

A reviewer in 1810 considered *The Yankey in London* "a very useless addition to the almost innumerable books of travels. . . ."[14] He attacks the young author (whose disguise at this point the reviewer has not penetrated) for failing to meet the proper people while in London. The reviewer concludes by commenting about the book, "There is a degree of smartness and some humour [but] . . . it gives nothing new, nothing but what a man, with some knowledge of English history, and the habit of reading English newspapers and magazines, might write in this country."[15] Ironically, the comment is more perceptive than the reviewer realized.

Thomas Pickman Tyler claims, "These letters really contain nothing which an intelligent Englishman . . . could justly regard as offensive."[16] He reports, however, that his copy of *Yankey* contained a note, "written no doubt by some irate Englishman. . . ." The note asserts, "This book is a lying libel, abounding with contemptible wit, malignant irony, malicious statements, and rascally deductions. . . ."[17] A twentieth-century critic, Constance Rourke, says that *Yankey* ". . . seems a precise account of fact and was generally taken for one. . . ." She adds, "The humor is keen, the style silvery-sharp: the little book is close to being a minor classic."[18]

Since Tyler had never been to England, where did the materials for *Yankey* come from? There are several possible sources. Travel abroad was not uncommon among upper-class New Englanders.[19] Tyler knew several people who had been in England, including his own brother,[20] the painter John Trumbull, Nabby Adams, and an acquaintance, Dr. Graham, who ". . . tells us all about London, and lies with the most traveled taste."[21] In addition, many books about England were available. It is ironic that Tyler, who writes about literary hoaxes in Letter XXXIII, is himself the creator of a literary hoax, *The Yankey in London*.

In the letter writer, Tyler has created a persona—a mask through which the real author speaks. Tyler has used a persona elsewhere: for instance, in the naive and candid Updike Underhill. The Yankey letter writer is so naive and so grave that the reader wonders whether Tyler is occasionally satirizing the character he has created, as he did with Colonel Manly in *The Contrast*.

Tyler also uses the Yankey to express some of his own ideas and interests. The young Bostonian is witty, extraordinarily well read, patriotic, and interested in human nature, language, literature, the law, and politics. The letter writer's wit can be seen in his amusing comments about the English climate (Letters XXIII and XLIII) or about slang (Letter XXX).

The young Bostonian seems to be extraordinarily well read. The number of literary figures referred to in *Yankey* reveals the breadth of Tyler's knowledge. The book mentions almost 100 different authors ranging from Aristotle, Horace, and Ecclesiastes through Shakespeare, Milton, and Joe Miller (of joke book fame). As would be expected, eighteenth-century English authors receive the largest share of attention. Dr. Samuel Johnson is mentioned the most frequently, with Joseph Addison second and Alexander Pope third. There are brief references to Steele, Cowper, Burke, Gibbon, and many others. Wordsworth and Coleridge, whose *Lyrical Ballads* first appeared in 1798, are not mentioned. *Yankey* also makes fun of stylized poetry (such as the Della Cruscan) and of the Gothic novel.

Tyler frequently encouraged native American literature. (See Letter XXXIII.) He also believed, as did many writers of his time, that literature should be *utile et dulci*, instructive and entertaining. (See especially Letter XI.) This idea is stated in the title of Tyler's late collection of miscellaneous writings, "Utile Dulci." A great deal can be learned from *The Yankey in London* about literary tastes at the turn of the nineteenth century.

Like Colonel Manly, the Yankey is a patriot. The Yankey praises American laws and government. At the end of Letter VIII he recalls ". . . that rational liberty for which our fathers successfully fought" (p. 45). There are also laudatory references to Washington, Adams, and the signers of the Declaration of Independence. The Yankey's patriotic attitude includes criticism of almost everything British. He is flattered by the English bookseller who says, "Sir, you were born in a new world; everything there evinces the vigour of youth: Europe, sir, I fear, is in her dotage" (p. 72).[22]

The letter writer enjoys observing the foibles of humanity. For instance, the American dandy abroad (Letter XLIV and the postscript to Letter XLV) is reminiscent of Dimple in *The Contrast*. The Yankey is amused by the fop's superficial behavior, as well as by his emphasis on fashion. In such works as *The Contrast* and "Epilogue to the Theatrical Season,"[23] Tyler commented unfavorably about people dominated by fashion. Another human foible is the reliance on medical quacks (Letter XLII). Tyler often attacked quackery, as in *The Algerine Captive* (Volume I, Chapters 19 and 20), in the essay "Fine Comb Points," in the report of the John Johnson case, and elsewhere.[24]

Tyler was deeply interested in language. This interest is shown in Letters XIX, XXX, and XLV. In *The Algerine Captive* (Volume I, Chapters 5, 7, and 14) Tyler had satirized classical education for its uselessness. In *Yankey*, the favorable attitude toward Greek and Latin led a modern critic to comment that Tyler had "recanted his earlier anti-classical bias."[25] However, Tyler was to echo his earlier views in Chapters VI and VII of *The Bay Boy (c.* 1824).

Another instance in which an opinion expressed by the letter writer conflicts with an opinion once expressed by Tyler is the attitude toward Lord Chesterfield. The Yankey cites Chesterfield as an authority on decorum (Letter XX). In *The Contrast* Tyler had excoriated Chesterfield's morals as well as those of anyone who followed Chesterfield's advice. Again Tyler may be satirizing the Yankey's gullibility.

Letter XLV contains a pioneering discussion of the dynamic qualities of language. The letter concludes that language ". . . will be subject to perpetual variance. New discoveries will call for new terms to express novel ideas. . ." (p. 177). This attitude toward changes in language is surprisingly modern.[26]

Yankey also reflects Tyler's interest in the law. Several prominent English legal authorities are cited. Letter VIII supports the rights of the common people and of landholders. Letter XLIII criticizes the propensity of the English government for "commercial aggrandizement. . ." (p. 154). Having foresaken urban Boston for rural Vermont, Tyler had become suspicious of cities and of mercantile interests. In 1808 Tyler wrote to his friend Senator Jonathan Robinson that America is not a land of merchants but of ". . . farmers and planters . . . and with them resides all the spirit we have as a nation. . . ."[27]

Although *The Yankey in London* frequently reflects Tyler's views, the book is a hoax. Tyler enjoyed fooling his friends, neighbors, and readers. In *Yankey*, he even has his persona comment sympathetically about other literary hoaxes.

The Yankey in London is the product of a clever pen. Tyler based his book upon the observations of other people, but he also expressed many of his own ideas in a pleasing and easy style. *Yankey* may or may not be a "minor classic,"[28] but it is an interesting, humorous book, a "tour de force" of comic invention.[29] *The Yankey in London* provides valuable insights into early nineteenth-century American attitudes.

CHAPTER 6

Miscellaneous Prose

ROYALL Tyler's miscellaneous prose includes sermons, speeches, law reports, and a variety of essays. These works show Tyler at his best and at his worst. In literature Tyler was a dilettante, a talented amateur who was especially adept at humor and satire. Despite his usual haste in writing and his lack of revision, Tyler had a prose style that was almost always felicitous. His style is characterized by the Neoclassical techniques of balance, parallelism, and climax. Like so many other eighteenth-century prose writers, Tyler was influenced by Joseph Addison and Richard Steele. In this chapter the most important, representative, and interesting of Tyler's shorter prose works have been selected for brief discussion.

I *Sermons, Speeches, and Early Essays*

A popular speaker, Tyler was invited to preach from various pulpits in Vermont. Mary Tyler recalls her husband's delivery of ". . . A most beautiful sermon, and orthodox for anybody."[1] Tyler once thought of entering the ministry, "but a consciousness of having lived too gay a life in my youth made me tremble lest I should bring in some way disgrace upon the sacred cause!"[2]

Only one sermon and one secular oration by Tyler are extant. "A Sermon and Prayer for Christmas Day" (1793) demonstrates the tolerant attitudes that are often found in Tyler's works: ". . . the good, the wise, the pious and the worthy are to be found among all denominations of Christians. . ." (p. 178).[3] America is referred to as ". . . the great day star from whence civil light and liberty is dispersed into all the benighted empires of the old world" (p. 184). George Washington is described as ". . . the uniting link that should bind the citizens of these United States in one federal bond of amity and peace" (p. 185). As might be expected, the sermon contains many biblical allusions and echoes.

The only surviving example of Tyler's secular oratory is "AN ORATION . . . IN COMMEMORATION OF THE DEATH OF General GEORGE WASHINGTON," delivered at Bennington, Vermont (February 22, 1800).[4] The oration itself is not an example of Tyler's best writing. The style and the emotions are forced: "That voice, which inspired us with courage in the hour of danger, shall no more be heard in the land. . ." (p. 273). Tyler continues to praise the late president: "Would you learn how to live? Read his life. Would you learn how to die? Visit his dying bed" (pp. 273-74). Despite the oration's effusiveness, the parallelism and balance of the style are at times impressive. No other examples of Tyler's orations are known to be extant.

More effective are the newspaper columns which Tyler wrote with his Walpole friend Joseph Dennie.[5] Dennie has been described as a "witty, aristocratic, critical personality."[6] Nathaniel Hawthorne said that Dennie was "once esteemed the finest writer in America."[7] In 1794, a series of original columns entitled "The SAUNTERER" appeared in the *Newhampshire and Vermont Journal* (predecessor of the *Farmer's Weekly Museum*). Apparently Dennie began the column and then asked his friends to make contributions. Four of the columns are signed "T," and may have been written by Tyler.[8]

"The SAUNTERER. No. V" (April 18, 1794) is the first of these columns to be attributed to Tyler. No. V is a leisurely essay about the differences among people: "Mankind, in their progress through life, may be aptly likened to a party of travellers, whose journey is directed to the same place, but who differ in their mode of travelling" (p. 291).

"The SAUNTERER. No. IX" (August 1, 1794) is signed "T." This column is about one of Tyler's favorite topics—tolerance.[9] The essay says, "As the world grows enlightened, religious toleration takes place; and political toleration must ensue from similar progress in knowledge" (p. 295). No. IX also laments "the existence [in America] . . . of the most rigorous slavery" (p. 295). Tyler may have contributed two other Saunterer essays. No. X (August 8, 1794) is a didactic statement about honesty. No. XI (September 5, 1794) discusses one of Tyler's pet peeves—clubs.[10] The Saunterer essays, in the tradition of Addison and Steele but without their polish, express amusement at human nature and a desire to reform human foibles.

II *Colon & Spondee*

The idea for Colon & Spondee was "the offspring of Tyler's prolific brain. . . ."[11] The first of this popular series of newspaper columns appeared on July 28, 1794, in the *Eagle, or Dartmouth Centinel.* Entitled "TO THE LITERATI" the essay was in the form of an advertisement for "*Mess.* COLON & SPONDEE, / WHOLESALE DEALERS IN / *VERSE, PROSE,* & *MUSIC.* . ." (p. 202). The shop sold "Salutatory and Valedictory Orations, Syllogistic and Forensic Disputations and Dialogues. . . . Bucolics, Georgics, Pastorals; Epic Poems, Dedications, and Adultatory Prefaces . . . Love Letters by the Ream. . . . Alliterations artfully allied—and periods polished to perfection" (pp. 202 - 203).

The columns included both poetry and prose. (Tyler's Colon & Spondee poetry is discussed in Chapter 7.) According to Joseph T. Buckingham, the Colon & Spondee items signed "C" for Colon were written by Dennie; items signed "S" for Spondee were written by Tyler; and "the poetical pieces . . . are all of his [Tyler's] composition."[12] When the anthology *Spirit of the Farmers' Museum* was issued in 1801, Joseph Dennie annotated his copy, indicating who had written the various selections.[13]

During the seven months that the Colon & Spondee columns were printed in the *Eagle,* only one prose piece marked "S" appeared (January 26, 1795). This work was under the heading of "*Miscellany.*" The short essay "*PRIME PUMPKIN!!*" is about a giant pumpkin vine that had to be destroyed after one of its branches choked a stand of maple trees and threatened an orchard (p. 205). The exaggerated story or tall tale was to become a staple of American humor.

In 1795, the Colon & Spondee series also appeared in Robert Treat Paine's *Federal Orrery.* Tyler's first contribution to the *Orrery* (January 22, 1795) was a single paragraph ("Amid the festivity . . .") which humorously commends George Washington's suppression of the "Pittsburg Insurrection," an uprising against federal economic policies (p. 206). On March 5, 1795, Tyler contributed a slightly longer piece ("Although to the man . . ."), which comments humorously on American public speaking (pp. 207 - 208).

In 1796, after a period of inactivity, the Shop of Colon & Spondee reopened in the *Newhampshire and Vermont Journal* (later called the *Farmer's Weekly Museum).* This periodical was first published by Isaiah Thomas and David Carlisle in Walpole, New Hampshire.[14] Joseph Dennie was editor from 1796 to 1799.[15] The paper's fame spread and its circulation lists grew to 2,000 with readers in all states except Georgia, Tennessee, and Kentucky. One of the subscribers was George Washington. The *Farmer's Weekly Museum* had a larger circulation "than that of any other rural paper in the United States."[16] As the century drew to a close, Tyler and Dennie were among the young nation's foremost men of letters.[17] They were the American Addison and Steele.[18]

The first Colon & Spondee column by Tyler to appear in the *Farmer's Weekly Museum* was entitled "The RUNNER, *or* INDIAN TALK" (August 9, 1796). This column contains several short items which indicate how ". . . *an* Indian *Editor might possibly publish a Paper. . .*" (p. 210). In this selection Tyler is tolerant about Indian customs and is mildly amused or satirical about the white man's foibles, such as the practice of dueling, which Tyler satirized in *The Algerine Captive.* Tyler also refers to Indians in "Fine Comb Points" *(Farmer's Weekly Museum,* April 11, 1797) and less favorably in "Sermon and Prayer for Christmas Day."

Tyler contributed sporadically to the Colon & Spondee series until 1802. The variety of topics covered in the Colon & Spondee columns demonstrates the breadth of Tyler's interests. Many of the essays deal with matters related to politics. Tyler's Spondee essay "*De* MINIMIS *curat Lex*" *(Farmer's Weekly Museum,* June 12, 1797) considers whether the will of the people should be expressed by "the voices of the majority" or whether "The minority ought, in all cases to carry the vote. . ." (pp. 219 - 20). Tyler developed the same idea in Volume I, Chapter 28, of *The Algerine Captive,* in an attack upon Thomas Paine.

Tyler's dislike of Thomas Paine is illustrated in the Spondee essays of August 25, 1797 ("*To our constant* CUSTOMERS *and the* PUBLICK"), April 17, 1798 ("PARAGRAPHS For The CHRONICLE"), and May 22, 1798 ("REMNANTS"). In the latter essay, Spondee accuses Paine of writing a "Vindication of the Character of Judas Iscariot. . ." (p. 239).[19] The essay of April 17, 1798, also criticizes Matthew Lyon, a Republican and Vermont's Representative to Congress (1797 - 1801). Like Paine, Lyon is the butt of humor in some of Tyler's poetry.

Another essay about politics was the only Spondee column to appear in Benjamin Smead's *Federal Galaxy* (September 9, 1799). The comic piece ("A PARABLE") is strongly Federalist. A story is told about some prisoners who rise together to "destroy their prison . . ." and build a new house (p. 250).[20] Soon, however, a mob begins to "pick away at the new building. . ." (p. 251). Spondee explains that the parable refers to those people who would pull down "a republican government erected by your own free consent" (p. 252). Tyler expressed an equally strong Federalist sentiment in a poem from 1797 entitled "The Sun and the Bats."

Tyler wrote about more than politics. A comic essay "ATTENTION, HAYMAKERS" in *The Spirit of the Farmer's Museum* describes folk beliefs about drinking.[21] Some haymakers are warned by Jotham Winrow not to indulge in "strong liquors" (p. 254). The haymakers are so impressed with the advice that they all "got tipsey by drinking the health of the wise Jotham Winrow" (p. 255).

Other comic pieces appeared over the years. The first Colon & Spondee column, "TO THE LITERATI," had been a comic advertisement (*Eagle*, July 28, 1794). A similar notice, headed "TO THE *PUBLIC*," with a second section headed "TO THE LITERATI," appeared in the *Farmer's Weekly Museum* on July 10, 1797. A certain "*JONATHAN DACTYLE . . . sells, by wholesale and retail,* . . . Quirks, Quibbles, Quillets and Quiddities . . . Puns, Jokes, Gibes, Witticisms. . ." (pp. 222 - 23). Colon & Spondee offer a $1,000 reward for Jonathan, who "BROKE his indentures, and [has] run away. . ." (p. 223). He took with him ". . . three Riddle Screws—One Sermon Vise . . . two Legislative Speech Echoes. . . . It is strongly suspected that this miscreant has forged a draught on the bank of Helicon" (pp. 224 - 25).

These light-hearted comments about the trade of writing show Tyler's awareness of literary conventions and his delight in parodying such conventions. A similar attitude is expressed in "The laudable rage, . . ." a Spondee column from the *Farmer's Weekly Museum* (February 18, 1799). Spondee notes "The laudable rage, for bringing science to the meanest capacity and purse. . . . Abridgements of Geography abridged; Treatises of Arithmetic, of the size of the adventures of Tommy Trip; and Grammers, as pleasing and as portable as Goody Twoshoes. . ." (p. 240). Spondee proposes a work entitled "THE PAP OF SCIENCE" which will include "GEOGRAPHICAL LULLABIES," "CYPHER CANDY," and "BIOGRAPHICAL BON BON" (pp. 240 - 41). Here Tyler satirizes the tendency to explain complex subjects in an overly simplified way.[22]

Tyler also used the Colon & Spondee series to satirize the Della Cruscan style of poetry. Della Cruscan poetry contains exaggerated elegance and inflated pretentiousness. Tyler mocks Della Cruscan excessiveness in several Colon & Spondee essays. "*Messrs.* COLON & SPONDEE *to their kind* CUSTOMERS" *(Farmer's Weekly Museum,* April 1, 1799) contrasts "far fetched" poetry with the "good homespun ware" of America (p. 244). Tyler had earlier appealed for a native American style in the prologue to *The Contrast* and the preface to *The Algerine Captive.*

On April 15, 1799, Spondee returned to the topic of Della Cruscan poetry with an essay beginning, "Although authors are. . . ." The essay describes Della Cruscan sonnets ". . . adorned with an ample arrangement of ambient alliteration; decked with a profusion of obsolete epithets, . . . replete with pleasing melancholy, soft despair, blissful woe, and heart rending happiness. . ." (p. 247; Tyler's satires of Della Cruscan poetry are also discussed in Chapters 5 and 7).

A Spondee essay headed "STATE OF LITERATURE IN ENGLAND AND AMERICA, AT DIFFERENT PERIODS" *(Farmer's Weekly Museum,* May 27, 1799) includes a letter from a man of wealth who has pretensions to learning:

> sur
> i wants to by sum Buks—as I am prodighouse fond of larnen. . . . (p. 249)

The Algerine Captive and *The Bay Boy* also contain examples of cacography (misspelling) used for humor.

Tyler wrote frequently about literature. He contributed three Colon & Spondee pieces entitled "An Author's Evenings" to the *Port Folio,* which Joseph Dennie edited from 1801 until his death in 1812.[23] The selection dated February 27, 1802, illustrates the breadth of Tyler's reading and interests. The columnist discusses writers that he likes. Among others, the Persian poet Hafiz is mentioned. In 1808 Tyler contributed three poetic adaptations of Hafiz to the *Port Folio.*

The last of Tyler's Colon & Spondee columns appeared as "An Author's Evenings" *(Port Folio,* May 15, 1802). In a reflective mood

Spondee begins, "I sometimes relax among books, as well as men" (p. 265). Stimulated by reading Lord Chesterfield (whom Tyler had pilloried in *The Contrast),* Spondee laments that proverbs "have so undeservedly fallen into disuse. . ." (p. 265). He compares Chesterfield's proverbs to those of Solomon in the Bible. This column was Tyler's last contribution to the partnership of Colon & Spondee. Tyler was elected to the Vermont Supreme Court in October 1801 and became increasingly involved with his career. Dennie often publicly exhorted his friend to ignore "judicial cares" and continue his writing,[24] but the partnership of Colon & Spondee had ended.

III *Other Essays*

Tyler was a prolific writer. Not all of his essays, however, can be identified. An essay "To the LOVERS of CIDER" *(Massachusetts Spy,* May 24, 1797)[25] has been attributed to Tyler because it is signed "U. Underhill." One of Tyler's miscellaneous contributions to the *Farmer's Weekly Museum* (June 26, 1797) can be identified from the markings in Joseph Dennie's copy of *The Spirit of the Farmers' Museum.* The selection, which is not a Colon & Spondee essay, purports to be the "SPEECH OF DAVID WOOD / *While standing in the Pillory at Charlestown, N.H. / May 27th,* 1797, *for forging a deed.*"[26] Wood explains in the speech that he sold "fifty acres of Vermont rocks" which did not legally belong to him (p. 302). He asks what the difference is between his crime and that of the great land speculators, especially the swindlers in Georgia. (In his play of 1797, *The Georgia Spec,* Tyler satirized the Georgia land scandals.)

Dennie's indications of authorship in his copy of *The Spirit of the Farmers' Museum* help identify eleven contributions by Tyler to the miscellany column of the *Farmer's Weekly Museum.* During the journal's publication, this column of "ANEXDOTES and JEUX DE MOTS" contained hundreds of brief items. The topics in many of these short pieces are favorite subjects for Tyler. One selection ("The bill for preventing . . .") refers to "the noisy and braggart Lyon" (p. 305) whom Tyler had satirized in "PARAGRAPHS for the CHRONICLE" (April 17, 1798). Another miscellany ("Perhaps the folly . . .") attacks "itinerant and imposing quackery" (p. 306). Tyler frequently inveighed against medical malpractice, as in the John Johnson case discussed below.

In 1803 a new weekly newspaper was issued in Brattleboro. The

Reporter was published by friends of Tyler—first by William Fessenden, and later by William's brother Thomas Green Fessenden. Within a month after the paper's founding, Tyler had contributed two poems to the publication. He also wrote four columns entitled "THE LUCUBRATIONS OF OLD SIMON." In the first of these columns (March 28, 1803), Old Simon explains: "*I am an Old Man, who have read, travelled and reflected, . . . but am now decently retired to my fire side and easy chair*" (p. 311). The essay then discusses history, politics, and literature.

The second Old Simon column (April 4, 1803) contains a playful essay about fashion (including a short poem), a discussion of "patience in adversity" (p. 313), a poem entitled "A Song. Old Simon," and a reflection upon Shakespeare's line "Sweet are the uses of adversity" (p. 315).[27] The third of the didactic Old Simon columns (April 11, 1803) consists of a series of questions selected from the work of the Puritan minister Richard Baxter, incorrectly referred to in the essay as Paul Baxter.[28]

The final Old Simon column appeared on April 18, 1803. Old Simon comments, ". . . the interest of true religion, and of our country are so blended and interwoven, that they cannot be well separated the one from the other" (p. 319). Old Simon is another of Tyler's masks—like Spondee, Updike Underhill, and the letter writer of *The Yankey in London*. Spondee is mildly sophisticated; Updike and the Yankey are naive; Old Simon is witty, widely read, patriotic, and philosophical.

In 1806 and 1807, Tyler contributed to Joseph Buckingham's magazine *Polyanthos*. Early in his career young Buckingham (under the name of Joe Tinker) had been an awestruck printer's devil on the *Farmer's Weekly Museum*. He idolized Tyler and Dennie. Tyler apparently was not aware at first that the editor of *Polyanthos* was the former printer's devil. When Buckingham was informed that the judge had praised his magazine, he began what was to be a fascinating correspondence between the two men.[29] Tyler promised (April 3, 1806) that he would ". . . occasionally furnish some original matter . . . some juvinile productions . . . the unvarying condition upon which you are permitted to publish it, must be your solemn promise, that I am not known as the author. . . ."[30] The Buckingham-Tyler letters reveal a great deal about literary life in early nineteenth-century America.

One of Tyler's contributions to *Polyanthos* was "a sheet of prose . . . divided into numbers, under the head of Trash. . . . I have been so long out of the fashionable world, that I doubt if I can hit the fashionable taste."[31] Four items under the heading of "Trash" appear in *Polyanthos*.

"TRASH . . . NO. I" (May 1806) begins with a lengthy anecdote explaining the title. "Some years since, visiting an old college acquaintance, I observed in his library a book, labelled . . . . 'TRASH' " (p. 414). The volume contained various pamphlets, ". . . the ephemeral productions of past time" (p. 414). Thus the series will be called "Trash." This essay also contains several comic items in prose and poetry.

"TRASH . . . NO. 2" (June 1806) is a poem, "The Town Eclogue."[32] "TRASH . . . NO. 3" (April 1807) is an essay about Jane Shore, the doomed mistress of King Edward IV of England. The final Trash column (May 1807) is also headed "NO. 3," but is actually the fourth of this brief series. Among other items, this last essay makes the point that literary critics ". . . are forced to discover some defects in order to evidence that we have some penetration" (p. 424). The critic is compared to the physician in *Don Quixote* who "criticised away the best viands" from the banquet table of the governor of Barrataria[33] (p. 424).

On March 6, 1817, Buckingham again asked Tyler for some essays. Tyler seems to have decided to write about his friend and collaborator Joseph Dennie, who had died in 1812. On July 10, 1818, an unsigned article appeared in *The New-England Galaxy*. The essay—headed "POSTUMI"—suggested a collection of Dennie's unpublished writings. On July 24, 1818, a second and final "POSTUMI" about Dennie contained an "Anecdote communicated by J.T.—" (p. 431). Buckingham credits the anecdote to Tyler.[34] The essay is a comic tribute to Joseph Dennie, describing his first speech in a court of law where the "unlettered" judge could not understand Dennie's elegant and learned plea (p. 435).

In 1817 Tyler submitted twenty-one essays entitled "SMALL TALK"[35] and eight other pieces to Simeon Ide's newspaper the *American Yeoman*, published in Brattleboro. The Small Talk essays cover a number of topics and frequently contain tall tales, puns, or anecdotes. Tyler may have written Small Talk essays about Spain's King Ferdinand (February 11, 1817), handwriting (March 18), attorneys (March 4 and March 25), intemperance (March 11 and April 8), Benjamin Franklin and British pronunciation (May 13), and numerous other topics. Some of the essays are about political subjects and national issues.

In 1817, Tyler apparently undertook to write a book for Simeon Ide. The title of Tyler's projected book was *The Touchstone; or a*

Humble Modest Inquiry into the Nature of Religious Intolerance.[36] Tyler had dealt with this subject before, especially in the early chapters of *The Algerine Captive*. Apparently *The Touchstone* was never completed. Ide writes, "I remember a large pile of printed sheets had accumulated. . . . What became of those sheets is more than I can tell. I am sure that I did *not finish* the book."[37] Ide describes the book as ". . . a very caustic and by no means '*dry*' commentary on the Beauties of '*Calvinism,*' '*Hopkintonianism,*' &c, &c."[38] A book entitled *The Touchstone,* thirty-six pages in length, was in the University of Vermont library at one time but has been lost.[39]

In January 1818, Simeon Ide announced that he was leaving Brattleboro. After Ide's departure, Tyler no longer had a local outlet for his material. Except for the two "POSTUMI" essays of July 1818, no more of Tyler's prose was printed during his lifetime.

IV *Cases at Law*

While Tyler was on the Vermont Supreme Court, the John Johnson trial was perhaps his most sensational case. John Johnson, a quack doctor, was treating Hannah Everts, who was insane. Johnson had the girl placed in a cage and gave her a large dose of opium mixed with rum. The girl died, and "there was some ugly evidence seeming to indicate additional criminality."[40] In 1805, Johnson was convicted of manslaughter, whipped, and fined. Public interest led Judge Tyler to prepare a report for publication. There is no clear evidence that the report itself was actually published, and no printed copy is extant. Thomas Pickman Tyler, however, reproduces the "Editors Address" (1805) which he says was "prefixed to the printed copy."[41]

Tyler's "Address" explains that legislation and medical licensing "do not restrain the unskilled from tampering with the health, limbs, and lives of the community . . ." (p. 406). The judge warns against trusting medical care to ". . . men of intemperate habits and profligate lives" (p. 407). Tyler frequently attacked medical quackery, as in Volume I, Chapter 19, of *The Algerine Captive*.

Another of Tyler's law cases is reported in a pamphlet from 1808: *The TRIAL of CYRUS B. DEAN. . . .*[42] This case is part of a complicated affair that aroused the emotions of Vermont citizens and elicited from Tyler a reasoned statement about the calm and equitable use of judicial powers. The Dean case (usually called "The Blacksnake Trial") is related to the turmoil which eventually led the nation into the War of 1812. The administration of Thomas Jefferson, beginning in 1807, had passed a series of embargo laws prohibiting trade with Canada. These laws cut off Vermont from such necessities as salt. Smuggling became common. The atmosphere was tense.[43]

In early August 1808, a patrol of militia attempted to capture the smuggler ship *Blacksnake*. Cyrus B. Dean, "the most daring and reckless" of the smugglers, led a stand against the troops.[44] Three militiamen were killed.[45] Eight smugglers were arrested, including Dean. Public opinion was divided concerning the incident. The Republicans called for the smugglers to be taken to "trial and execution as murderers in cold blood. The Federalists palliated their [the smugglers'] conduct. . . ."[46]

At the trial, Judge Tyler gave the charge to the grand jury.[47] He reminded the jurors that the government "secures to every man retribution for individual wrong. . ." (p. 408). Tyler stated the court's awareness that ". . . on every side the angry and intolerant passions are excited. . ." (pp. 408 - 409). He also stated the court's determination that the defendants, "though prejudged by the popular voice, will have a candid and impartial trial. . ." (p. 409). Tyler cautioned the grand jurors, ". . . divest yourselves of all these prejudices and partialities which so readily attach to us in private life. . . . if you are assailed by hatred or malice; by fear, favor, affection or hope of reward, repair to your oath" (pp. 410 - 11). Tyler's charge reflects the ideals of the American legal system.

The grand jury indicted the smugglers for murder. Cyrus Dean was tried, found guilty of murder, and executed, ". . . the first instance of capital punishment in Vermont."[48] The other smugglers were sent to prison. Aware of the intense public interest, Tyler edited the court records for publication. In *The TRIAL of CYRUS B. DEAN* . . . , a forty-eight-page pamphlet which gives the arguments of the various attorneys, Tyler wrote a lucid account of a complicated situation.

At times, Tyler was equally lucid in the two-volume *Reports of Cases Argued and Determined in the Supreme Court of Judicature of the State of Vermont*, issued under Tyler's name by the New York publisher Isaac Riley. Volume I was issued in 1809, and Volume II in 1810. (Riley also published Tyler's *Yankey in London* in 1809.) Tyler's correspondence with Riley is a valuable illustration of the negotiations between an author and his publisher.

Tyler received an inquiry from Riley in the autumn of 1808 about the possibility of issuing a collection of law reports. Tyler replied, ". . . ever since I have been upon the bench, now nine years, I have been collecting reports of decisions in the Supreme Court . . . in this State. . . . Upon liberal encouragement, I shall be willing to vend the copy right. . . ."[49] Tyler asked for "one hundred and twenty dollars" when Riley had received the first 100 pages of material.[50] The *Reports of Cases* was the last book-length work by Tyler to be published during his lifetime and one of the few works to be published under his name.

In the law reports Tyler compiled more than 100 cases that were settled by the Vermont Supreme Court during the years 1800 to 1803. His work on these reports is more an example of editing than of writing. Each case is presented with a précis, the main arguments of the attorneys, the verdict of the court, and other pertinent evidence and information. Footnotes, occasionally lengthy, explain the precedents and references, as well as the implications of the court's decisions. Each volume begins with an alphabetical listing of the cases contained within the volume, and each ends with an index arranged alphabetically by the type of case. The comments made by Tyler and recorded in the *Reports of Cases* display a keen legal mind, an ability to reason carefully, an understanding of the law—its history and precedents—and a humane attitude.

Three appearances by Tyler as a defense attorney are recorded in the *Reports*. In one of these appearances, the case of the State against IS.S. (June Adjourned Term, 1801), Tyler defended a man who challenged another man to a duel. Tyler's client was acquitted because he sent a "*Written Challenge*. The various modes of disturbing or breaking the peace . . . are manifestly those of verbal abuse. . . ."[51]

After Tyler joined the court, he served on a case which was in its own way a forerunner of the more famous Dred Scott case of 1857. The case before the Vermont court was intricate. In 1783 Stephen Jacob, an attorney, had purchased a slave woman named Dinah. She worked for Jacob "until some time in 1800 when she became infirm, sick and blind. . . ."[52] At this point Jacob denied responsibility for the woman, and she became a public charge. The Selectmen of Windsor brought a legal action against Jacob, claiming that Dinah belonged to him and that he should therefore provide for her.

The case began in the Windsor County Court, whose presiding judge at the time was Stephen Jacob himself. Jacob does not appear to have disqualified himself from the case. The Selectmen lost on a technicality and appealed to the supreme court of the state. Ironically, by the time "Selectmen of Windsor against Stephen Jacob, Esquire" reached the supreme court, Jacob had become assistant judge on that court. He disqualified himself from sitting at the appeal.

The case was heard by Chief Justice Robinson and Assistant Judge Tyler at the August 1802 term. Tyler wrote the opinion, a masterpiece of legal tact. Tyler asserted that the case must be judged not on national grounds but according to "the construction of our own State constitution . . . [which] does not admit the idea of slavery in any of its inhabitants. . ." (p. 394). Tyler stated that ". . . when the master becomes an inhabitant of this State, his bill of sale ceases to operate here" (p. 393). Over fifty years later Chief Justice Roger B. Taney of the United States Supreme Court would hear a similar case and issue a completely different opinion.

The law reports generally won praise. In 1810 William A. Palmer, later governor and senator from Connecticut, had written about the *Reports of Cases*, ". . . they are not only accurrately, but elegantly reported."[53] A Vermont colleague of Tyler's, R. C. Mallory, later a United States Representative, wrote, "To the lawyer of taste . . . It will afford a rich entertainment."[54] A negative comment came from John Savage of the New York Supreme Court, who said in 1825, "Tyler's Reports are not considered good authority, even in his own state."[55] Despite this comment, Tyler's law reports are easily read and valuable for reference.

Tyler's association with Isaac Riley also resulted in other projects. On May 22, 1810, Tyler wrote to Riley, "I have been sometime engaged in collecting materials for an American Law Dictionary."[56] Riley referred the Law Dictionary to some lawyers. Nothing more is known about this project.

A different idea discussed in the same letter did come to fruition. Tyler sent to Riley "the manuscript of a little Treatise upon the nurture & management of Infants . . . written by an American Lady."[57] This "little treatise" was Mary Tyler's *The Maternal Physician*,[58] published by Riley in 1811. It is one of the first American books about infant care.[59] *The Maternal Physician* contains advice about diet, dress, discipline, and treatment of diseases. Often practical and sometimes unintentionally amusing, the book provides valuable insights into early nineteenth-century American family life, customs, and folk medicine. Dr. James Thatcher, a Revolutionary War physician and early historian of American medicine, described the author as "a facinating American writer" and "sensible." Thatcher said the book was "a production replete with interesting matter, and worthy the attention of every nursing family."[60]

V "*Utile Dulci*"

A few years after the *Reports of Cases* was published, Tyler lost his position on the Vermont Supreme Court. Shortly after this defeat, he became ill. As Tyler's illness progressed, the family attempted to maintain his interest in writing. Tyler's son Edward encouraged his father to gather together his "fugitive pieces of merit" for possible publication.[61] Apparently Tyler took this advice. On April 19, 1825, Mrs. Tyler noted in her diary that a friend was assisting them with a manuscript: "Mr. Williston set out for New York and carried with him the Manuscript of *Uteli Dulci* a collection of Dramas, Fables—Tales &c. &c.—designed for the use of Children and Youth . . . to get published on the best terms he can. . . ."[62]

On May 15, 1825, Mrs. Tyler wrote to Edward, ". . . my opinion is that your Father's name alone would insure a sale of one Edition of that work. You forget that he is not unknown as an Author. Many of his old friends know his merits as a Poet, altho from many adverse circumstances justice has never been done to his productions. . . ."[63] Little is extant from "Utile Dulci" except the title page, the "Introduction to the Sacred Dramas," the three sacred dramas themselves, an essay about marriage, two fables for children, and several poems. (The sacred dramas and the fable "The Tale of the Five Pumpkins" are discussed in Chapter 3; the poems are discussed in Chapter 7.) At the bottom of the title page of the manuscript is the famous quotation from Horace which recommends *Utile Dulci*—to combine in literature the useful and the sweet, the instructive and the delightful (p. 438).

The essay entitled "Marriage" in "Utile Dulci" may be from Tyler's younger years.[64] The writer gives practical advice to the clergyman who is looking for a helpmate. The essay begins, "*Let your courtship be brief*" (p. 444). One piece of advice may have been based upon Tyler's own experience with Nabby Adams and Mary Palmer: "*Chuse a woman who has been humbled but not lower'd by family misfortunes*. . . . The young woman whose family has been exposed to great misfortunes, learns more of the world . . ." (p. 451). The next suggestion is: "*Chuse a woman of strong good sense and great prudence*" (p. 452). Finally Tyler advises the young clergyman: "*Let her have some taste for books, less passion for dress and the most genuine relish for the duties of domestick life*" (p. 452). Tyler frequently wrote about women and about the qualities of a good wife.[65]

The other prose remnants of "Utile Dulci" have a long history. In 1799 Tyler wrote the Boston publisher Joseph Nancrede that he was working on a children's book of "Moral Tales."[66] Nancrede and Tyler became involved in several months of negotiations. The Tyler-Nancrede letters of 1800 are a remarkable example of the relationships between a writer and his publisher. Nancrede apparently set type for the book of "Moral Tales." If any copies were printed, they have not survived. Mary Palmer Tyler says that her husband's *Tales for Children* "were purloined by a dishonest publisher some years after, but the rough drafts of many of them are still in my possession."[67] There is no way to determine whether Mrs. Tyler's reference is to Nancrede. Tyler also offered Nancrede a cosmography (a universal geography) and a comic grammar.[68] Apparently nothing came of these projects.[69]

The compilation of "Utile Dulci" was one of the last literary projects undertaken by Tyler. The selections are uneven in quality, but they do include materials which provide insights into the writer and his times.

The prose writings of Royall Tyler cover a variety of topics, ranging from comic essays to learned legal reports. This chapter about Tyler's work has briefly discussed a representative selection of Tyler's non-fiction prose writings. Constance Rourke says, "Tyler achieved polished prose, neat verses and satire with the best of them."[70] Tyler's style has been described as "easy, graceful and elegant. . . ."[71] Many of Tyler's fugitive pieces are still worth reading today, the work of a literate man who was a clever and effortless writer.

CHAPTER 7

Poetry

ROYALL Tyler's "poetical effusions . . . were for the most part, brief 'Coups d'esprit' struck off at the leasure moments of a busy life . . . [works] which he never thought it worth while to correct and polish."[1] Joseph Dennie describes Tyler as "determined to Lope-de-Vega it and write 100 lines upon one leg. . . ."[2]

A hasty writer, Tyler was not a poetic genius. But he was a clever person, skilled in the writing of verse. Tyler's poetry forges no new paths. It uses the standard content, styles, and forms of the late eighteenth and early nineteenth centuries. The poetry of Royall Tyler reflects the literary movements of his times, both in England and America.

Tyler's poetry also reflects the life of his times. Like his prose, his poetry is rich in local color and extols the values of native American literature. The poems frequently comment on women and marriage, the theater, patriotism, politics, and literature. Tyler's verse does not always exhibit the lively style and mischievous wit that distinguish some of his prose. Nevertheless, Tyler's poetry deserves more attention than it has yet received. A selection of the more important, interesting, and representative poems of Royall Tyler will be examined briefly in this chapter.

I *Early Poems*

According to Tyler's family, he ". . . wrote verse and prose from his college days. . . ."[3] Four early manuscript poems,[4] not published until the twentieth century, are in the collection of the Boston Public Library. Each of these poems is simply entitled "Song." The first is a bouncy piece: "There was a jolly Cobler / Who lived in Boston Town. . ." (p. 3). The second is about a merchant apprehensively awaiting the return of his ships (p. 4). The third ("Oh like a Storke") contains a series of similes (p. 5). The fourth is about "*foaming Flip*," a sweetened malt drink (p. 5).

Another manuscript poem, "A Prologue to Be Spoken by Mr. Frankley," is at the Vermont Historical Society. This poem may have been written during Tyler's Harvard days. Its heroic couplets urge dramatists to discourage vice and to portray "The road to virtue. . ." (p. 6).[5] Tyler agreed with the classical and eighteenth-century ideal that literature should be *utile et dulci*, instructive and delightful.

Teaching a lesson was an important element of Tyler's writing. One of Tyler's manuscripts contains a didactic poem, "The Colt" (*c.* 1796). The charming verse says that a child needs to be groomed as carefully as a colt, "Not for the good he *can* do now, / But *will* do when he's grown up" (p. 50).[6]

Apparently, Tyler's first publications were the *May Day in Town* lyrics (1787), and *The Contrast* (1790). His first published poem appeared as a pamphlet in 1793.[7] "The Origin of Evil" is unique in the Tyler canon. It is about ". . . the *fall* of *Eve* and *Adam*. . ." (p. 12). Adam and Eve are described as "Innocent of nuptial blisses . . ." (p. 13). Then their temptation is depicted. The two are "Blushing and panting with desire. . ." (p. 14). They sin, ". . . gorged with bliss" (p. 14). Finally, ". . . there's the FALL!" (p. 15). "The Origin of Evil" is effective in its sensuous imagery. It seems to be Tyler's only erotic poem.

On January 6, 1794, Tyler contributed "A Christmas Hymn" to the Hanover, New Hampshire, *Eagle*. The hymn, one of Tyler's first newspaper poems, begins, "Hail to the joyous day . . ." (p. 18). This poem, with minor changes, was later reprinted in a broadside which described the authorship: "Composed by Royall Tyler, Chief Justice of the State of Vermont."[8] This is one of the rare instances in which Tyler's name was attached to his work. Tyler contributed several other poems to the *Eagle*. "Ode to Night" (July 14, 1794) demonstrates that Tyler, who could mercilessly satirize inflated poetry, was at times subject to the same faults. The poem begins, "Hail Reverend Monarch! Hoary Night!" (p. 16).

Tyler's comic poetry made its first published appearance in the *Eagle* (August 11, 1794). "Anacreontic to Flip" is a good-humored work, a drinking song. Flip is an alcoholic beverage. Tyler wrote again on the topic of drinking in "Original Epitaph on a Drunkard" (*Farmer's Weekly Museum*, June 19, 1797), a poem about "stammering, staggering, boozy Joe. . ." (p. 61). Tyler also praised libations in "A Song / *Suitable for the Season*" (*Farmer's Weekly Museum*, December 10, 1798): "*Drain the glass, the goblet drain, / Drown awhile each sorrow. . .*" (p. 82). Tyler's attitude toward drinking is usually lively and amused. Only in his poem "The Chestnut Tree" does he warn against the dangers of drink.

II *Poems about Women*

Women were frequent topics in the poetry of Royall Tyler. A poem about female virtues, "The Sensitive Plant: A Fable," appeared in the *Eagle* on July 21, 1794. A letter from William Coleman (Aaron Burr's law partner) requesting a copy of *The Algerine Captive* also asks, "Please add the 'Windsor Eulogy' and 'The sensitive plant' . . . Col. Burr . . . is to be delighted with this. . . ."[9] Tyler's son comments that "The Sensitive Plant" was written in "a style, then in vogue, but now . . . far out of fashion."[10] The poem uses Tyler's favorite meter, iambic tetrameter, in quatrains rhyming ABAB. It is a didactic work praising the twin virtues of sensitivity and modesty. The didactic purpose of the poem is lightened by its tone.

Tyler describes a good wife in "The Rural Beauty, A Village Ode" (*Eagle*, August 25, 1794). The poem contains a conventional description of nature and also provides information about rural clothing of the time: "Her raven skirt and sash of blue, / Her stockings white, and coal-black shoe. . ." (p. 29). The simplicity of the poem is enhanced by the frequently irregular tetrameter rhythm and by the use of rhymed couplets, with half-rhymes such as "strewn" / "alone."

A different type of woman is described in "Almoran to Eliza / *With a Heart of Ice*" (*Eagle*, September 22, 1794). Here the "man of sentiment" is advised to choose "A sentimental wife" (p. 32). Tyler had dramatized this idea earlier in the characters of Maria and Manly (*The Contrast*, 1787).

Tyler occasionally pokes fun at marriage. "The Test of Conjugal Love" (*Eagle*, December 29, 1794) reverses the classical story of Alcestis. Tyler's comic poem is about Strephon, who is dying. His grieving wife begs Death to spare her husband, threatening that if he dies she will go with him "to the grave" (p. 35). When Death appears and asks who calls for him, the wife replies, ". . . why who should it be? / *But the gentleman there on the bed*" (p. 35).

"The Bee, *an Epigram*" (*Federal Orrery*, February 23, 1795) makes another satiric comment. In a pastoral setting, Strephon woos the coy Delia.[11] When Strephon compares himself to a bee seeking sweets, Delia replies, "Your very metaphor's repelling, / For should my Strephon dart love's sting, / I fear, like bees, *he'd raise a swelling*" (p. 39). Tyler sometimes enjoyed using double-entendre.

In "The Clown and the Rose. A Fable," Tyler again discusses female virtue. This Spondee poem was published in Joseph Dennie's *Tablet* (August 11, 1795) and was republished in the *Farmer's Weekly Museum* (February 14, 1797, and January 26, 1801). Young Laura is protected by "Thorny Virtue" (p. 41) until she will marry a young man "And in his bosom shed her sweets" (p. 42). The poem's didacticism and use of personifications are a heritage of eighteenth-century English poetry.

Tyler's "Choice of a Wife," a Colon & Spondee poem (*Newhampshire and Vermont Journal*, December 6, 1796), is both humorous and serious. The potential lover is advised to "shun the proud, disdainful eye," for Nature "made the eye proclaim the mind" (p. 49).

"A Reputation Vindicated" (*Farmer's Weekly Museum*, April 11, 1797) is a verse anecdote about "A bachelor of forty-five" who is seeking a wife. Invited to woo his neighbor's daughter Sue, the bachelor replies, "What little Sue, why she's too green, / The girl has not yet seen sixteen" (p. 54). The father vindicates the girl's reputation: "She's old enough to be your lady, / For *two years past, she had a baby!*" (p. 54). In "Epigram" (*Farmer's Weekly Museum*, September 25, 1797), Spondee admonishes prospective bridegrooms, "Ye fools, if you were buying houses / . . . [you'd] try the house with one night's lodging" (p. 67).

In "Alliterative Address" (*Newhampshire and Vermont Journal*, March 14, 1797), Tyler wrote about women:

> Fair Fanny's fame shall flourish far,
> Till teazed time shall, toiling, tire;
> And Daphne, Delia, Dorcas dear,
> Shall fail to fan fierce Fancy's fire. (p. 51)

Joseph T. Buckingham comments, "Tyler was extremely fond of amusing himself and others with specimens of his skill in alliteration."[12] The poem is a tour de force of technique.

In a Spondee verse "To Miss Flirtilla Languish" (*Farmer's Weekly Museum*, May 1, 1798) the poet satirizes Flirtilla's use of rouge, her braided hair, her ruffs and spencer (a tight jacket or bodice). These details provide a picture of some of the fashions of the time (pp. 79 - 81).

"Spondee's Mistresses" *(Farmer's Weekly Museum,* April 15, 1799) is a charmingly didactic poem. It is distinguished by "an air of unstudied ease and elegance, which are seldom seen in the productions of those, who write for newspapers. . . ."[13] In imitation of Abraham Cowley's *The Mistresses* (1647), Tyler has produced a lively satire on the relationships between men and women.[14] A dapper beau has wooed a girl who almost broke his heart—"MISS CONDUCT"; a lame girl—"MISS CHANCE"; and a thoughtless girl—"MISS TAKE" (pp. 85 - 86). The hapless suitor is finally visited by "MISS FORTUNE." She "With bony fist, now slaps my ears, / And brings me to my senses" (p. 86).

Tyler's real preference seems to have been for women who have simplicity and learning. (See the essay "Marriage," discussed in Chapter 6.) A manuscript poem "Say is it Height or Shape or Air," praises the woman "Whose mental beauties . . . e'en the fairest make more fair" (p. 226). Another poem, "Horace, Ode XXII, Lib. I" *(Polyanthos,* June 1806), describes a woman immune to the frivolities of fashion: "She who alone her native charms relies on, / Needs not the aid of rouge, ceruse, or carmine. . ." (p. 149).

Tyler wrote a comic poem about fashion for Buckingham's *Polyanthos* (April 1807). "Epigrammatick Sketch" depicts an anxious husband who is rushing to bring a new bonnet to his wife before it goes out of style: "I must hasten to my true one, / The fashion else I fear will alter, / And my Duck will want a new one!" (p. 159). In this poem, the use of feminine rhymes ("true one" / "new one") increases the humorous effect.

One of Tyler's last printed poems, "The Inimitable Fair," (Brattleboro *Farmer's Weekly Messenger,* June 24, 1822) praises a woman whose "elegant mind, by learning refin'd, / Lends a lustre to beauty's exterior. . ." (p. 182). These were the qualities of Tyler's ideal woman.

Despite occasional comic moments, Tyler is often serious about marriage. In an early Spondee poem, "The Properties of a Good Wife" *(Farmer's Weekly Museum,* May 6, 1799), Solomon comments, "Who can a virtuous woman find, / Whose beauties sparkle in her mind. . ." (p. 88). This is an echo of Proverbs 31:10, "Who can find a virtuous woman? for her price is far above rubies. . . ." Tyler is gravely serious in this poem, as he usually is when he deals with a biblical topic, and as he frequently is when he discusses the qualities of a good wife.

III *Poems about the Theater*

Once Royall Tyler had moved to Vermont in the early 1790s, he was far from the theatrical scene, "except a straggling play wanders hither. . . ."[15] But Tyler never lost his interest in the drama. For a production of Oliver Goldsmith's *She Stoops to Conquer*, which played in Charlestown, New Hampshire, Tyler wrote an "Occasional Prologue," published in the *Federal Orrery* (December 29, 1794). This is one of the few poems containing Tyler's name as the author—"*Written By / R. Tyler, Esq.*" (p. 36). The poem encourages Americans to write so that "native actors [will] speak our native lays" (p. 37).

While John Steele Tyler was manager of the Federal Street Theatre in Boston, Royall Tyler wrote for his brother a long poem (118 lines) entitled "An Occasional Address." This piece appeared in the *Federal Orrery* (November 9, 1795). As in his "Occasional Prologue," Tyler uses rhyming iambic pentameter couplets. "An Occasional Address" combines two of Tyler's favorite themes—patriotism and a plea for native culture. The poem calls for a time "When bards shall carol on our river's side, / And *Charles* shall rival British *Avon's* pride. . ." (p. 45). In a letter to Joseph Dennie, Tyler called the prologue "a meagre thing—";[16] he was not being unduly modest.

Theater continued to fascinate Tyler. A comic "Epigam" (p. 65) about the stage appeared in the *Farmer's Weekly Museum* (July 24, 1797). Another poem, "Epilogue to the Theatrical Season," appeared in Joseph T. Buckingham's *Polyanthos* (April 1806). "Epilogue" is in heroic couplets (rhymed iambic pentameter couplets), a favorite eighteenth-century meter. This is Tyler's second-longest poem (244 lines). "Epilogue" begins:

> The season's clos'd, the benefits are o'er,
> And heroes, heroines, strut the stage no more. . . .
> Theatrick lords, whose pride no power could stem,
> Are dwindled down to *very common men;*
> And royal dames, who erst the pit could charm,
> Now wash old laces, or old stockings darn. (p. 134)

The poem discusses the actors of the previous theatrical season and comments on their performances.

According to Thomas Pickman Tyler, his father's poem "excited very general interest, and especial wrath in those who were most severely handled and still greater indignation in those who were not noticed at all."[17] "Epilogue" is one of Tyler's most skillful newspaper poems, written in an easy and graceful style. A month later, another poem by Tyler about actors appeared in *Polyanthos* (May 1806). "Love Varses to the Bucheous Daffodel" mocks the dialect of an actor on the Boston stage.[18]

"An Epistle to My Muse, *Or a Postscript to the Epilogue to the Theatrical Season*" (*Polyanthos*, June 1806) attacks actors for failing to play their parts and for trying to attract the audience's attention. Tyler mocks "The blundering actor, whom old Shakespeare drew: / See-saws the air, and swells, and struts, and brags, / And kicks and tears a passion into rags" (p. 153).[19] "An Epistle to My Muse" is a clever and energetic satire, more biting than is usual for Tyler. According to Thomas Pickman Tyler, "Epilogue" and "Epistle" depend ". . . mainly for their interest on the passing events of the year."[20] "Epistle to My Muse," however, rises above the moment to make a comment upon the vagaries of actors in all eras.

The Bay Boy, Tyler's late unfinished novel, also contains a poem about the theater. The chapter entitled "First Theatrical Representation in Boston" is introduced by a poem in iambic tetrameter couplets, "Come, Thalia, with thy comic smiles. . . ."[21] Far removed from the theater, Tyler nevertheless maintained his interest in the stage.

IV *Patriotic Verse*

Tyler frequently responded to special occasions by writing poetry. One of Tyler's earliest poems for a public event is also one of his best. "Ode Composed for the Fourth of July" originally appeared in the *Newhampshire and Vermont Journal* (July 19, 1796). The poem has been frequently reprinted, even in the twentieth century.[22]

Early Americans were vigorous in celebrating Independence Day. Tyler describes one Fourth of July celebration in a letter to his wife.[23] For another such celebration, Tyler was called upon to read the Declaration of Independence. Tyler reports that, amid the "hilarity," the explosion of a cannon caused a number of injuries and one death.[24]

In the tetrameter verse of "Ode Composed for the Fourth of July," Tyler captures the holiday's energetic spirit: "Squeak the fife, and beat the drum, / INDEPENDENCE DAY has come!!" (p. 47). The poem describes the tempting foods being prepared: the roasting pig, cockerel, nutcakes fried in butter, pumpkin and apple sauce, brandy, and maple sugar. Tyler also uses the occasion to make a paradoxical antislavery statement:

> Sambo, play and dance with quality;
> This is the day of blest Equality.
> Father and *Mother* are but men,
> And Sambo—is a Citizen. (p. 47)

The "Ode" attacks the French Jacobins and the American Republicans, but concludes happily: "Thus we drink and dance away, / This glorious INDEPENDENT DAY!" (p. 48). The excitement of July 4 is portrayed in Tyler's most frequently reprinted poem.

Tyler also attacked slavery and praised liberty in his novel *The Algerine Captive* (1797). For example, the description of the Algerian slave market (Volume II, Chapter 2) is preceded by a four-line verse from the "AUTHOR'S *Manuscript Poems*":

> Despoiled of all the honors of the free,
> The beaming dignities of man eclipsed,
> Degraded to a beast, and basely sold
> In open shambles, like the stalled ox.[25]

This is a vigorous use of blank verse.

Tyler was active during the Fourth of July celebrations in 1799. He wrote five poems for the occasion—three odes for delivery at different villages, and two Fourth of July songs. The best of these odes was the "Windsor Ode, *Written by R. Tyler, Esq. and sung the 4th of July,* 1799" (p. 97). First published in the *Farmer's Weekly Museum* (July 29, 1799),[26] "Windsor Ode" has been called "a good specimen of the author's poetry. . . ."[27]

"Windsor Ode" is predominantly in iambic tetrameter. Four of the six stanzas use the same refrain:

> Shout! shout Columbia's praise,
> Wide through the world her glory raise,
> Our Independence bravely gain'd,
> Shall full as bravely be maintain'd. (pp. 97 - 99)

The other two refrains are a variation of this one. The refrains are more musical and lively than the stanzas. "Windsor Ode" attacks the "Atheist rod" of the French and praises the Federalist leaders: "Great Adams" and "Brave Washington" (pp. 98 - 99).

Similar topics—patriotism, dislike of the French,[28] and praise for Washington and Adams—are found in "Walpole Ode" *(Farmer's Weekly Museum,* July 15, 1799) and "Westminster Ode" *(Farmer's Weekly Museum,* July 22, 1799). "Westminster Ode" praises village life, industry, and simplicity (pp. 101 - 104). Assuming that the three odes for the Fourth of July were all written in the same year, they are a remarkable production. The poetic quality of the odes, however, leaves much to be desired. These poems exemplify Tyler's haste and the lack of revision in his writing.

The two songs that Tyler also wrote for the Fourth of July 1799 add to the picture of a facile versifier who took little trouble with his writing. Joseph T. Buckingham liked Tyler's "Convivial Song / *Written by R. Tyler, Esq. and sung at Windsor, on the evening of the* 4*th of July. . ."* (p. 104).[29] This song was published as a broadside (possibly in 1799),[30] and also appeared in the *Federal Galaxy* (July 22, 1799). Like his drinking songs and the "Ode Composed for the Fourth of July" (1796), Tyler's "Convivial Song" is rhythmic and energetic.

> Come fill each brimming glass, boys,
> Red or white has equal joys,
> Come fill each brimming glass, boys,
> And toast your country's glory. . . . (pp. 104 - 105)

Both "Convivial Song" and "Patriotic Song / *Written by R. Tyler, Esq. . . ." (Federal Galaxy,* August 26, 1799) praise Washington and Adams, and promote patriotism.

"Love and Liberty / *By R. Tyler, Esq." (Port Folio,* October 20, 1804) combines patriotic and romantic themes. The poem contains bird imagery, as in the refrain: "Love fills their throats, / Love swells their notes, / Their song is Love and Liberty" (p. 125). The poetic skill of this poem shows considerable advance over that of the partisan verses of 1799. "Love and Liberty" is one of Tyler's better poems.

Tyler also wrote a poem about George Washington. "The Mantle of Washington" is undated and was not published until the twentieth century.[31] "Godlike Washington" (p. 176) is dead, but he is asked to ". . . cast thy earthly mantle down. . ." (p. 177). This poem is weak, forced in sentiment, monotonous in rhythm, and lacking in tonal unity. Much of Tyler's patriotic verse is flawed and undistinguished.

V *Local-Color Verse*

Tyler's verse—like his prose—often describes the customs, fashions, foods, and beverages of New England. Two poems give particular insights into New England life. "Specimen of a Poetical Paraphrase of Our General's Journal" was printed in the *Farmer's Weekly Museum* (June 3, 1799). With vivid details, the poem describes the market at Roxbury and the tricks used by farmers to make their products appealing: "Some skim the old, some water the new milk: / Some with distended cheek inflate the lamb, / Some with dishclout plump the kidnies cram. . ." (p. 94). Tyler returned to the subject of the marketplace in "The Town Eclogue," printed as part of the Trash series in *Polyanthos* (June 1806). There are similarities in subject matter, but "Specimen of a Poetical Paraphrase" is the far more lively production. Both "Specimen" and "The Town Eclogue" depict the sights, sounds, and smells of a New England market.

The headnote to Chapter XV of *The Bay Boy*, "Thanksgiving and Christmas Days," contains a wealth of local-color descriptions, including that of holiday foods and customs:

> Plumbpudding, turkeys, roast and boil'd,
> Brant, fowl and geese both tame and wild,
> Custards and tarts and whips froth'd high,
> And last not least the pumpkin pie.

The poem refers to the Twelfth Night cake with its "hidden bean." The antics of mummers are described, and the merry-makers are reminded to feed the "Hungry poor. . ." (p. 234).[32] Tyler often does well at describing convivial scenes. In "Thanksgiving and Christmas Days," he recreates the gaiety of pre-Revolutionary Boston during the festive season.

VI *Satiric Poems, Mainly Political*

Tyler's poetry praises his heroes, such as Washington and Adams, and attacks his foes. Tom Paine, for instance, is a frequent target of Tyler's humor. In *The Algerine Captive*, Chapter 29 of Volume I is about Paine's *Age of Reason*. This chapter is headed with one of Updike Underhill's original poetic creations: ". . . While wretched

Paine, to 'scape the bloody strife, / Damns his mean soul to save his meaner life" (p. 73).[33] Paine is also attacked in the poem preceding Chapter 21 of Volume II of *The Algerine Captive.*[34] Here Paine is described as writing in a manner "fluent, false, and vain" (p. 75).

Another favorite target for Tyler was Matthew Lyon, Vermont's Republican congressman. In "A New Song" *(Farmer's Weekly Museum,* June 26, 1797), Tyler mocks the congressman's Irish origins and dialect. Lyon is also attacked in "Vauxhall Gardens" *(Farmer's Weekly Museum,* March 13, 1798).

Until about 1807, Tyler was ardent in defending Federalism and opposing the Democratic-Republican party. One of his poems, inspired by Aesop's fables, is a satire on the political clubs of the Democratic-Republicans. "The Sun and the Bats, &c. A Fable" appeared in the *Farmer's Weekly Museum* (October 2, 1797). An earlier Saunterer essay (September 5, 1794) had expressed disdain toward "clubs or societies. . . ."[35] A similar attitude underlies the satire of "The Sun and the Bats." The poem describes ". . . how certain bats, / In a dark hole, like Democrats, / Held a fraternal club. . ." (p. 67). The sun, representing the Federalists, smiles on the animals of darkness, "As Adams smiles with dignity. . ." (p. 69). Then "the solar president" praises ". . . this land which gave you birth, / The favourite spot of all the earth. . ." (p. 70).

"The Sun and the Bats" extols village simplicity, religion, and industry. Tyler uses his favorite poetic form, iambic tetrameter couplets, for this strong partisan statement, which is more an attack than a satire. As in Tyler's comments about Thomas Paine, "The Sun and the Bats" demonstrates that Tyler had the ability, rarely used, to be an effective polemicist.

Tyler mocks exclusive clubs in "Irregular Supplicatory Address to the American Academies of Arts and Sciences" *(Farmer's Weekly Museum,* April 25, 1797). This poem describes scientists who are engrossed in the minutiae of learning. Tyler also criticizes useless learning in *The Algerine Captive* and *The Bay Boy.*[36]

VII *The Della Cruscan Satires*

The Della Cruscan style has been called part of "a rash of bad taste that broke out in English poetry between 1787 and 1791. . . ."[37] This school of poetry is associated with Robert Merry (1755 - 1798), an Englishman who during a visit to Florence was initiated into the Academy Della Crusca (Academy of the Chaff), founded in 1582 to purify the Italian language. In turn, Merry tried to purify his native tongue by writing pompous and elevated poetry signed "Della Crusca." The style spread quickly across the Atlantic "and threatened to ingulf everything that was true, simple, and genuine."[38]

Boston, always alert to English fashions, was quickly infected. The American "tendency toward flamboyant example" has been called "the Boston style."[39] In England Della Cruscan extravagance was satirized by William Gifford. In America two Hartford Wits, Richard Alsop and Theodore Dwight, burlesqued Della Cruscan poetry in several issues of the *American Mercury* (Hartford, Connecticut, 1791). The Della Cruscan style was a natural target for Royall Tyler's mischievous wit.

Tyler's mimetic talent is apparent in his parodies of this extravagant poetic mode and its overly emotional state of mind known as sensibility. The poet's wit enabled him "to detect and detest the fashionable literary follies."[40] Joseph Dennie wrote that Tyler's was "the first real broom in America . . . raised against the fantastic school."[41] When Tyler began to mock Della Cruscan style, Colon & Spondee were at the height of their popularity. Tyler's satires were widely circulated. These satires have "as much cunning as the *Baviad* [of William Gifford] and less malice, more glee and less savagery."[42]

Tyler's first Della Cruscan satire appeared in the *Farmer's Weekly Museum* (April 4, 1797). Entitled "An Ode to a Pipe of Tobacco," the poem is "*Addressed by Della Yankee to Anna Jemima.*"[43] The meter is iambic tetrameter, with a varied rhyme scheme dominated by rhyming couplets. Tyler has written a mock love poem to his pipe, that "extatic tube" (p. 52). Since his love for Anna has ended, his only consolation is the pipe: "My lips shall press no other lip, / Than its red, pouting, balmy tip. . ." (p. 53).

Tyler again mocked Della Cruscanism in the *Farmer's Weekly Museum* (May 16, 1797). His "Address to Della Crusca" has been called "devastating" and "extraordinarily clever satire. . . ."[44] The poem, which is signed "DELLA YANKEE," describes the extravagant style of Della Crusca, and then pleads,

> Come mighty conqueror, thy foes disperse;
> Let loose "thy epithets," THOSE DOGS OF VERSE; . . .
> Rise, Della Crusca, prince of bards sublime,
> And pour on us whole cataracts of rhyme. (pp. 60 - 61)

The final couplet indicates Tyler's real opinion: "Proclaim thy sounding page, from shore to shore, / And swear that sense in verse, shall be no more" (p. 61).

Tyler's skillful use here of the heroic couplet, frequently with a caesura (a meaningful pause in the middle of the line), his mock-heroic attitude, and his diction—particularly in the last line—are all reminiscent of Alexander Pope's satires, especially *The Dunciad* (1728, 1743). "Address to Della Crusca" is Tyler's most effective satire on Della Cruscan effusiveness.

Another satire, "Sonnet / To the INDIAN MUCKAWISS . . . ," appeared in the *Farmer's Weekly Museum* (September 11, 1797). The poem is ". . . *humbly attempted in the manner of* CHARLOTTE SMITH," an English Della Cruscan writer (p. 66). The poem begins with an apostrophe to the Whippoorwill: "Child of the sobre eve, whose sad delight. . ." (p. 66). A note at the end of the poem explicates—and emphasizes the foolishness of—the opening lines: "*Who ever thought, except a poet, that a Whippoorwill had the eve for its mama. But why 'sober eve?' Why? Because eve keeps good hours, goes to bed early, and never gets drunk*" (p. 66). The note—which is signed "SENSIBILITY"—goes on to praise the use of oxymoron in the words "sad delight." (Oxymoron is a figure of speech which yokes together two contradictory terms, such as "blissful woe.") The note says of the poem, ". . . *There is something in it so delightfully woeful that a mind of sensibility will sink into a pleasing melancholy under the operation of it*" (p. 66). Sensibility's explanation, which itself contains two additional examples of oxymoron, is a masterpiece of satire.

The final Colon & Spondee satire on Della Cruscanism appeared in the *Farmer's Weekly Museum* (April 15, 1799). An "Advertisement" explains that Colon & Spondee can "brighten the dullest compositions in prose and verse, by the apt and judicious insertion of capital letters, italics, asterisks. . ." (p. 86). To demonstrate their handiwork, Colon & Spondee present "Sonnet to the Turtle Dove," perhaps Tyler's most extravagant Della Cruscan parody. A few lines can exemplify the humorist's style.

> OFFSPRING OF GRIEF! child of EXTATIC woes!
> NOW *night* sheds soft her curtain'd sleep,
> AND *greedy* wealth, and vulgar *bliss* REPOSE,
> And only sorrow JOYS to wake and weep. (p. 87)

These lines mock the Della Cruscan use of capital letters and italics, the exaggerated nouns and adjectives, the oxymorons, and the excessive sentiment. In *Yankey in London* (1809), Tyler again mocked the Della Cruscan style.[45] His poetic satires have been called "the first influential reaction against Della Cruscanism. . . ."[46]

VIII *Imitations*

Tyler satirized some poets and imitated others. He was a skillful literary mimic whose poetic range is effectively demonstrated by the verses he wrote under the influence of foreign writers—Scottish, Norse, even Persian authors. For example, Tyler's interest in language led him to employ Scottish dialect in one Spondee poem, "The Exile" *(Farmer's Weekly Museum,* May 20, 1799). Spondee, using the conceit that his shop manufactures verse upon request, explains, "We ha' lately set up a Caledonian Loom, in which we're gawn to weave Scottish Web. . ." (p. 91).

Tyler tried to imitate early Norse bards in "The Scandinavian Hero" *(Port Folio,* April 20, 1805). The poem is set in Valhalla, where the hero sits "amid the carousing gods" and drinks mead from skulls (p. 129). More effective are Tyler's imitations of the Ossian forgeries of James Macpherson.[47] Tyler's "Versification of a Passage from Ossian" *(Port Folio,* April 20, 1805) uses iambic pentameter couplets.

> The northern blasts thy cloudy gates unfold,
> Thy warlike form, O Fingal, I behold;
> Amid the curling glooms that wrap thee round,
> Appear thy gleaming arms in fight renown'd. . . . (p. 129)

The final lines of the poem are among Tyler's more effective atmospheric descriptions. The poet addresses the hero Fingal:

> But when thou comest forth in calmness sweet,
> The gales of morning play around thy feet . . . ,
> The bushes shake their green heads in the breeze,
> The roe toward the distant desert flees.[48] (p. 130)

This passage has an appealing directness and simplicity.

The *Port Folio* of May 11, 1805, contained "Versification of a Dialogue from Ossian," four quatrains of iambic pentameter, rhyming ABAB. Again Tyler effectively creates the mood: "The storms are hush'd, the pelting showers pass, / Serene and tranquil is the noon of day. . ." (p. 130). Apparently the example of Macpherson inspired Tyler.

In 1808 Tyler submitted to Joseph Dennie's *Port Folio* three odes in imitation of the Persian poet Hafiz. The first "Ode From Hafiz" was published on March 5, 1808. It contains eight iambic pentameter quatrains, rhyming ABAB. Less effective than Tyler's Ossian imitations, the first ode is a studied piece of verse. Tyler does, at times, achieve an easy elegance: "Shiraz, to thee I pour the votive song, / And greet thy towers; lovely city hail! . . ." (p. 171). The second "Ode From Hafiz" *(Port Folio,* March 26, 1808) is intricate in form and contains an ironic description of the narrator: "Ah! where's the sense I once could boast? / Alas in wine and love all lost. . ." (p. 173). The poem expresses well the concept that life and happiness are fleeting.

The third "Ode From Hafiz" *(Port Folio,* April 16, 1808) has eight quatrains of iambic pentameter, rhyming ABAB. Like other Eastern poetry, such as that by Omar Khayyám and Rumi, the topics are wine, roses, love, and mutability: "Fill high again! pour, pour the wine I prize / To haste the moment of expected bliss" (p. 174). The influence of Hafiz upon Tyler is fortuitous. Only in "The Origin of Evil" was Tyler as successful in creating sensuous descriptions.

IX *Miscellaneous Verse*

Tyler's verse ranges over many topics, including religious and philosophical commentary, praise of nature, and some poems which defy classification. Tyler extolls Christian fortitude in two of his poems, "Ejaculatory Sonnet" *(Port Folio,* July 11, 1801)[49] and "A Song. Old Simon."[50] The latter is a semicomic description of the acceptance of infirmities. "Hymn to the Supreme Being" *(Reporter,* March 28, 1803; and *Port Folio,* May 21, 1803) is a religious poem that is monotonous in sound and conventional in statement.[51] Tyler's interest in the ministry is expressed in a 26-line poem entitled "Extract from 'The Divine,' a Poem in Six Books" *(Polyanthos,* April 1806).[52] Using blank verse, Tyler extolls the virtuous man of the cloth who devotes his life to helping people.[53]

In "By Science Aided" *(Polyanthos,* April 1806), the optimistic ideas are similar to those expressed in Pope's "Essay on Man" (1733). Tyler's narrator speaks about a work on astronomy and how it affects him: "One powerful law through all extends its force, . . . / And in bright order forms th' harmonious whole" (p. 132). Tyler refers to the natural world again in "Ode to the Humming-Bird" *(Port Folio*, March 23, 1805). The mixed images—"Thou insect bird! thou plumed bee!" (p. 126)—are not successful.

Late in life, Tyler published another nature poem, "To the Moon" *(Farmer's Weekly Messenger*, November 4, 1822). Six quatrains of iambic pentameter rhyming ABBA praise the "Queen of the night." Tyler writes, "Lonely and pensive I delight to stray," and "A soft and tranquil calm pervades my soul. . ." (p. 188).[54] Tyler's late poetry is frequently melancholy.

A manuscript poem dated 1797 makes a comment on Tyler's profession. In "Epigram on Seeing a Pair of Scales in a Lawyer's Office" one of the characters concludes cynically that the scales are "A sign that justice *there is sold*" (p. 76).[55]

A singular work entitled "A Riddle" was published in the *Reporter* (February 21, 1803). The editor promised to print the riddle's solution, but did not do so. The nine-quatrain riddle begins: "I never was, nor yet I am; I never spake, and yet I talk. . ." (p. 122). Whatever Tyler had in mind for this poem remains a mystery. No single answer seems to fit every verse.

In *c.* 1824, "A Valedictory Address" was printed as a broadside. "Valedictory Address" was later reprinted in Henry Burnham's *Brattleboro, Windham County, Vermont.*[56] The poem was "*Delivered . . . at the Quarterly Examination of Miss Peck's Select School, by Thomas Pickman Tyler,—(Aged Eight Years)*" (p. 189). It makes monotonous use of iambic tetrameter, mainly in rhymed couplets but with some alternating rhymes. The young speaker is shown some "shrivel'd" seeds from which will grow beautiful flowers (p. 190; the image of the "misshapen seed" is also used by Tyler in "The Chestnut Tree"). The girls in the school are then compared to the lovely flowers that will grow from the seeds.[57] "Valedictory Address" is not a particularly effective poem, but Tyler does manage to capture the sound of his youthful narrator's voice.

X *Melancholy and Death*

Another of the topics found in Tyler's poetry is death. "Elegiac Ode" *(Columbian Centinel*, June 15, 1799) is a formal lament. The poem uses the popular Neoclassical technique of personification: ". . . *Peace* her olive branch displays," and ". . . *War*'s brazen trumpets bray. . ." (p. 96). "Elegiac Ode" is conventional in style and sentiment.

A five-line stanza by Tyler appeared at the top of the obituary section in William Fessenden's *Reporter* from March 28 to June 27, 1803. Headed "Obituary," the stanza is attributed to "Underhill's Poems." The first of the unrhymed and irregular lines proclaims, "He comes! the awful King of terror comes!" (p. 121). The influence of such Graveyard poets as Edward Young, one of Tyler's favorite authors, is evident here. Despite the strained elegance of "Fever, appoplex, in horrid phalanx march" (p. 121), Tyler rose above his usual poetic level when he used the voice of Updike Underhill.

Tyler's "Elegy / *Occasioned by the death of the Rev. Samuel Stillman,* D.D. . . ." *(Polyanthos,* April 1807) also shows the influence of the Graveyard School: "Oh, Death! fell tyrant of a ruined world. . ." (p. 155). "Elegy" demonstrates Tyler's respect for the clergy, who are "affliction's constant friend. . ." (p. 157). Another example of the influence of the Graveyard School can be found in "Ode to Friendship" *(Port Folio,* August 15, 1807). The first two stanzas are conventional statements about friendship. In the third stanza the tone changes as the narrator asks for "one friend to mourn me in the grave" (p. 166). The request is reminiscent of Thomas Gray's popular "Elegy Written in a Country Churchyard" (1751).

Less melancholy was Tyler's final contribution to Dennie's *Port Folio,* "Impromptu to a Young Lady Playing" (April 16, 1808). This poem has some similarities to John Dryden's "Alexander's Feast" (1697). In Tyler's poem the narrator compliments a young lady by saying that if Timotheus—a famous musician—were alive, she would win the prize for music from him (p. 171). The poem goes on, "You seem an angel to our eyes, / We think ourselves in heaven" (p. 175). With this brief selection of 1808, Tyler's poetry disappears from print for more than nine years.

On November 11, 1817, a Brattleboro journal, the *American Yeoman,* printed a melancholy poem, "November," by Tyler. At this time, the poet no longer had a national audience. He was old and ill and impoverished. "November" reflects this dismal situation:

A few days past the fields were green,
And every beauty might be seen; . . .
But now, alas! the scene is changed,
And nature almost seems deranged. . . .
And such is man—his prime today,
To-morrow sees him swept away. (pp. 178 - 79)

The monotonous quality of the rhythm, however, detracts from the seriousness of the subject.

In 1822, Tyler had a burst of literary activity, publishing nine poems in local newspapers. The repetition of certain subjects and images in the poems suggests that these ideas were significant to Tyler. Several of the poems are somber in tone. References to melancholy and death are found frequently in Tyler's later verse. In "Memory" *(Farmer's Weekly Messenger*, September 2, 1822), the narrator reviews his youthful years of "joy and hope." Now he can only look forward to "substantial rest" (p. 183). The reliance of this poem on stylized devices, such as the personification of "Mem'ry," makes it more stilted than "November." But "Memory" does present a vivid picture of the thoughts that may have occupied the poet's mind in his declining years.

The poem "Evening Hour" *(Bellows Falls Intelligencer*, September 2, 1822) combines autobiographical references and melancholy (pp. 184 - 85). "Pastoral Song.—(Written in June.)," which appeared in the *Farmer's Weekly Messenger* (September 16, 1822), is conventional in its sentiments about "departing day" (p. 186).

The first five stanzas of "Solitude" ("Lone Spirit") in the *Farmer's Weekly Messenger* (September 30, 1822) are reminiscent in topic, diction, and iambic tetrameter meter of John Milton's "Il Penseroso" (*c.* 1631). At the end of Tyler's poem the narrator asks to be guided to "that heav'nly road, / . . . which leads to God. . ." (p. 187). In "Stanzas to****" *(Farmer's Weekly Messenger*, October 21, 1822), the narrator portrays himself as "he, whose spring-like years are o'er. . ." (p. 187). The emotions described in these late poems are conventional; the language is stilted and often trite. Nevertheless, the poems seem to reveal Tyler's attitudes.

The last of the nine poems appeared in the *Bellows Falls Intelligencer* (November 18, 1822). The poem is entitled "Solitude," but its tone is quite different from the previous "Solitude" ("Lone Spirit"). The *Intelligencer* poem begins, "Happy the man who lives retir'd, / Far from the noisy scenes of life . . ." (p. 188). The ideal expressed here is that of *otium*, satisfaction with the simple, especially the rural, pleasures of life.[58] The nine poems that Tyler published in 1822 are interesting but not particularly distinguished.

Except for "A Valedictory Address" (*c.* 1824), no other poems by Royall Tyler were published during his lifetime. However, a typescript in the Vermont Historical Society contains what might be Tyler's last poem, "The Splendour of the Finest Lyre. . . ." Tyler's authorship of this poem is disputed.[59] The verse was found written inside Tyler's copy of *The Works of . . . Lord Byron*, Vol. II, which was published in New York in 1825. The book's arrival in Vermont must have been surprisingly prompt, for the poem (possibly in Mrs. Tyler's handwriting) is dated "Feb. 21, 1825." The poem's statement that "British hearts" will remember Byron (p. 237) seems unusual for Tyler. However, the punctuation (especially the use of dashes), the references to the lyre (see Tyler's "Stanzas to****"), the melancholy tone, and the religious ending are all characteristic of Tyler's late poetry—and of verses by innumerable Romantic writers. If Tyler wrote "The Splendour of the Finest Lyre," its last lines are a fitting conclusion to his poetic works: "Sleep till Eternity shall break / The slumber of the grave!" (p. 237).

XI "*The Chestnut Tree*"

In the preface to *The Bay Boy* (*c.* 1824), Tyler refers to "my rhymes on the chestnut tree."[60] He then quotes from the poem a seven-stanza description of an antiquarian scholar. A letter from Mary Palmer Tyler to her son Edward (May 15, 1825) provides a clue for the dating of the poem: "As to the Chestnut Tree it merits being printed by itself. . . ."[61] Apparently Tyler had completed "The Chestnut Tree" sometime before May 1825. The poem remained in manuscript, however, until a limited edition was printed in 1931.[62]

Tyler's last major poem contains some vivid characterizations and descriptions. It is sentimental, but not mawkish. The poem is Tyler's longest and his most interesting. The version printed by Péladeau—"The Chestnut Tree; or a Sketch of Brattleborough East Village, At the Close of the Twentieth Century . . ." (p. 194)—is 756 lines in length, arranged into 189 quatrains of iambic tetrameter, rhyming ABAB. The poem contains twenty-three brief vignettes about the villagers.[63]

The opening lines may provide an autobiographical reference: "Misshapen seed! thy uncouth form, / Thy rough exterior, . . . / Provoke the careless gazer's scorn. . ." (p. 194).[64] The seed is planted by the narrator, who realizes that he will be dead before the tree reaches full growth. The narrator then looks to the future, "The vista of two hundred years" (p. 196). This statement suggests that the poem will recount events in the early twenty-first century, but the subtitle and line 167 refer to "the Twentieth Century. . ." (pp. 194, 199). Possibly the poem is set in the late eighteenth century of Tyler's youth rather than in the early 1820s. Possibly the poem was started or completed earlier than the 1820s. Internal evidence for dating seems to be inconclusive.

The beginning of the poem briefly lists various people who will enjoy the tree's shade in the future—beaux, shy girls, elderly women, playful boys, and others. It is "As if some theatre display'd / Life's varied, shifting, empty scene" (p. 197). The vignettes follow, many of them in contrast to each other.

The first portrait describes the beau and the flirt, who do not change with time. The next vignette describes a high-spirited and impudent village "Hoyden." She is a "romping, tricksey pest, / Whom all must love, and none approve" (p. 198). The focus shifts to a group of young people gathered around a book showing "fashions for the present year" (p. 199). The girls laugh, exclaiming, " 'What monstrous frights our grandames were!' " (p. 199).

This disparaging attitude toward fashion, which is frequently expressed in Tyler's work, gives way to a scene of pathos as the ailing and the elderly come to the tree. These people suffer from dropsy, palsy, consumption, and (in another possibly autobiographical reference) "Corroding cancer. . ." (p. 199).

Again the tone changes as Tyler portrays two physicians arguing over a patient on his deathbed (p. 200). The narrator then observes two friends walking arm in arm. Only an hour ago they had been "engaged in verbose war." The two men are lawyers, who are "only foes, when richly fe'd" (p. 200). The next two stanzas depict a gambler, "His fortune, fame, and pleasure fled" and only "Despair" remains (p. 201; a late manuscript fragment, "Gambling," expresses a similar attitude—see p. 227).

In contrast, the eighth section describes the simple love of a Quaker couple. "A household God is nuptial love; / His Lares shun the public gaze. . ." (p. 202). The scene changes quickly, as "The beastly drunkard staggers by. . . ." Six stanzas portray the inebriate, his condition "worse than madness. . . ." He is a "wilful, lingering suicide" (p. 202). In Tyler's earlier works, the writer seemed to be amused by drinking; here he disapproves.

The tenth vignette describes the "athletic play" of children (p. 203). The tone and subject here, as elsewhere in the poem, are reminiscent of Oliver Goldsmith's "The Deserted Village" (1770). The eleventh section depicts the fisherman who "holds on high, with pride sublime, / A glorious string of speckled trout" (p. 205). The narrator considers fishing "solace for a vacant mind. . ." (p. 203). In the next section, the narrator is less sympathetic with the hunter (a "cruel sportsman"), whose victim "bleeds his little life away" (pp. 203 - 204).

In the thirteenth portrait, the poem exhibits a social awareness that is rare for its time. In ten stanzas the cast-offs of the industrial age are described. They are "impoverish'd wanderers" condemned "To want, to beggery, and to sloth." The laborers perform "the same unvarying task." Their wages are "scanty"; their lives lead "To penury and neglected age." The narrator laments that the laborer's children will be "Bereft of education . . . / While tatter'd garments, meagre fare, / Stunt and deform the starv'ling race" (p. 204).

Tyler's indignation leads him to write some of his most powerful critical lines:

> Ah barbarous system! cruel trade;
>   By art infernal sure design'd
> At once to torture and degrade,
>   To starve the body and the mind. (p. 204)

The poem then makes a statement that seems to prophesy about obsolescence, automation, oversupply, and unemployment:

> Some new machine's ingenious art
>   The laborer's tardy work supplies,
> Or o'erstocked market's glutted mart
>   Their wonted task to them denies. (p. 204)

Deprived of employment, the laborers may turn to "vice or beggary . . ." or to "the Town's cruel charity" (p. 205). This unusually realistic section ends optimistically: "Blest be our age! and blest our Land! / Whom yet no scenes so foul degrade. . ." (p. 205). In the thirteenth section of "The Chestnut Tree," Tyler assumes the role of social prophet and social critic, foretelling the blight of industrialism.[65]

The next fourteen stanzas present a more cheerful scene. From the tree one may look toward the nearby mountains and watch a youthful group of climbers enjoying themselves. In the fifteenth section, "A female pauper now appears" (p. 207).[66] Perhaps the dying Tyler was thinking about his own wife when he described this good woman, once charitable to her neighbors, whose "earthly bliss in ruins lies" at the death of her bankrupt husband (p. 208).

The sixteenth section is a portrait of a "Stale bachelor of forty two" (p. 208).[67] The sentimental description of the lonely bachelor may be autobiographical in its reference to the approach of "deafness, blindness, grief and pain" which "Mark life's last, lingering wintry stage. . ." (p. 209; compare this poem to Tyler's "The Widower," p. 33). By way of contrast the next section depicts a young married couple and their children: "With married bliss and love elate. . ." (p. 210).

The eighteenth section presents a different aspect of marriage. This section contains a sentimental description of a widowed mother. Like the depiction of the female pauper, this characterization may be based on the dying writer's awareness of his own situation. The husband's death is portrayed with pathos and sentimentality, including his plea that his children be cared for.

The poem's most delightful portrait follows. A "meagre, studious wight" appears, garbed in "antique coat and vest. . . ." The subject is an antiquarian scholar who gleefully reads a "worm-eaten, smoak-dried page. . ." (p. 212). The narrator wonders what the scholar is studying:

> In sooth! it is the manuscript
> Of this poor feeble verse of mine,
> Which in despite of taste and wit
> Has straggled down to future time. (p. 212)

The "Bookworm" gloats over the manuscript, "Not for its worth, but for its age." He reads "The spelling quaint, the line perplext . . ." and "in the margin gravely notes / A thousand meanings, never meant" (p. 212). This comment on literary scholarship is witty and penetrating.[68]

The next portrait is of another scholar, a "studious young divine. . ." (p. 213). In the twenty-first section, a "pensive" group of people go to the local cemetery. The sentimental scene appears to have been influenced by the Graveyard School of poetry.[69] There are no poetic surprises in this section. Conventional images are used, as in "A tott'ring, ruin'd monument." The cemetery contains the grave of the "*earliest village pastor,*" who is described with Tyler's usual respect for clergy as "the *best of men*" (p. 214).

When night falls, the chestnut tree is visited by "Two youthful lovers sighing vows" (p. 215). Then the final section of the poem gives way to melancholy. The narrator mentions his own "furrow'd brow, and tresses gray. . . ." He laments that "Invention's gone, and fancy fled, / And naught but chiming rhyme remains" (p. 215). The alliteration and assonance in these lines emphasize the meaning. The narrator asks for a moral lesson that will be appropriate to his "waning years" (p. 215). Autobiography, sentimental clichés, and religious consolation are combined in the poem's concluding section:

> Misshapen seed! I too like thee
>   Shall in our parent earth be cast,
> And with new life shall quicken'd be
>   When the grave's wintry season's past. (p. 216)

The narrator hopes to "mount" to heaven and to "Bloom in Immortal verdure there" (p. 216).

"The Chestnut Tree" has all the faults associated with Tyler's poetry—careless meter and ineffective rhyme, stock sentimental phrases, insistent pathos, and frequent didacticism. Nevertheless, "The Chestnut Tree" contains some remarkable and interesting portraits: the merry hoyden, the pompous doctors and hypocritical lawyers, the simple Quaker couple, the female pauper, and the dusty antiquarian. These perceptive vignettes are written in some of Tyler's most effective verse. Especially remarkable in the poem is the pioneering social commentary about the dregs of industrialism. Section thirteen is noteworthy because its descriptions of the horrors of the industrial age come so early in American literature.[70]

"The Chestnut Tree" can be considered as a summary of Tyler's poetic characteristics and as a summary of the characteristics of the literary periods through which he lived—the late eighteenth and early nineteenth centuries. This poem deserves far more attention than it has as yet received. One of Royall Tyler's last poems, "The Chestnut Tree" is also one of his best poems.

This chapter has discussed a selection of Royall Tyler's more important, interesting, and representative poems. Much of Tyler's poetry demonstrates technical skill as well as lack of effort. Joseph T. Buckingham describes how Tyler wrote his Colon & Spondee poems ". . . with a dash of the pen, seldom taking any pains to revise them. They are noted for inaccuracy of rhymes . . . but they are remarkable for sprightliness of thought and expression, and an easy flow of language. They embraced topics of all sorts, local and general, temporary and permanent, and were well charged with wit and humor."[71]

Even Tyler's son, Thomas Pickman Tyler, criticizes his father, who "wrote verse with ease, and rapidity; often with too little attention occuring of Rhyme or Measure; striking off his conception in the heat of the moment."[72] A late nineteenth-century critic, S. Arthur Bent, echoes Buckingham, saying that Tyler's poems are "noted alike for the sprightliness of their thought and the inaccuracy of their rhymes."[73] In 1928 a Vermont commentator explained, "Tyler is seldom the poet . . . but he is a fluent and dexterous versifier with much skill in parody and mock heroic. His sensitive ear catches readily the tunes of other men. . . ."[74]

Tyler's verse is frequently derivative, and he does not always improve on his sources. Usually, his topics are traditional and his ideas conventional. The rhythms are sometimes monotonous and the rhymes awkward. Despite these flaws, however, Tyler's poetry—especially the early verse—often has an appealing spirit and buoyancy.

The poetry spans two literary periods. Tyler's earlier poems clearly show Neoclassical influences. His later poems are more personal, more melancholy. Possibly this change is a result of Tyler's own experiences; possibly Tyler's later poetry was influenced by the early nineteenth-century Romantic poets, such as Lord Byron.

A few of Tyler's poems are memorable: the sensuous "Origin of Evil," the sprightly "Ode Composed for the Fourth of July," the clever Della Cruscan satires, the poetic headnotes by Updike Underhill, the local color in "Specimen of a Poetical Paraphrase," the Scandinavian and Persian poems, the first section of "The Wolf and Wooden Beauty,"[75] and "The Chestnut Tree." In such poems, the Man of Law proved himself also to be a Man of Letters.

CHAPTER 8

Conclusion

THROUGHOUT much of his life, Royall Tyler insisted on anonymity as an author. He once cautioned Joseph T. Buckingham not to reveal his name, "either by private communication to your friends or any public hints to the patrons & subscribers."[1] This request was not based on modesty. As John Quincy Adams had once explained in a letter to Joseph Dennie: ". . . worthy citizens . . . [are] convinced that it is impossible to be at once a man of business and a man of rhyme. . . ."[2]

Such attitudes did not encourage careful writing and rewriting. Joseph Dennie had once asked Tyler to: ". . . give me your Royal word not to write a play in less time than I have dictated this sentence." Dennie added, "I exhort you to industry. . . ."[3] Tyler rarely heeded Dennie's exhortation. He was a hasty and careless writer. Despite this lack of polish, Tyler's work is important in American literature.

Tyler's play *The Contrast* (1787) was the first American comic drama to be performed by professional actors in the United States. *May Day in Town* (1787), now lost except for the recently discovered lyrics to the songs, was apparently America's first musical play. *The Algerine Captive* (1797), one of the nation's earliest novels, contained the first fictional portrayal of life in New England and was one of the first American novels to be published abroad. This novel contains an early attack upon the institution of slavery, a subject to which Tyler often returned as writer and jurist.

Tyler wrote on many other subjects, including the dynamics of language. His satires attempted to reveal the foibles of his countrymen and to improve their manners. Tyler also was dedicated to the development of native American literature. His local-color descriptions of New England customs in *The Algerine Captive, The Bay Boy* (*c.* 1824), and in some of his essays and poems are valuable sources of information for students of American life. Colon & Spondee, begun in 1794 and written with Joseph Dennie, was one of America's first newspaper columns.

But Tyler is of interest for more than historical reasons. Several of his works are worth reading in themselves. *The Contrast,* America's first comic drama, is a comedy of manners that—when well produced—can still entertain audiences. "The Origin of Evil" (1793) is a subtly suggestive poem. Volume I of *The Algerine Captive* contains interesting depictions of life in pre-Revolutionary New England. The revision of *Captive* as *The Bay Boy* is even more interesting.

Catherine Rourke described *The Yankey in London* (1809) as a "minor classic."[4] The satires in the Colon & Spondee series, especially the Della Cruscan parodies, are sharply original and clever. *The Island of Barrataria* (written after 1813) is an amusing dramatic adaptation from Cervantes. "The Chestnut Tree" (*c.* 1824) is an effective poem, particularly in the sections about the problems that will be caused by industrialization.

Tyler's influence as a humorist was probably greatest in *The Contrast.* Subsequent writers imitated his play. William Dunlap, James Nelson Barker, Anna Cora Mowatt Ritchie, and others borrowed liberally from *The Contrast.* The stage Yankee, created by Tyler in *The Contrast,* is still a comic type in our times.

Tyler's work had other influences. James Fenimore Cooper once commented that Tyler in *The Algerine Captive* was one of the "early and authentic historians" of this nation.[5] Long after Tyler's death, local-color effects, such as those he had used in *Captive,* were an important characteristic of American fiction. Devices used by Tyler—comic letters, misspellings, dialect, and exaggeration—were to become staples of American humor. Tyler's emphasis on the encouragement of native American literature can also be found in such nineteenth-century writers as Ralph Waldo Emerson and Walt Whitman. Tyler's work is part of the mainstream of American literature.

Tyler wrote with enough skill to be called "the genius of the Walpole group. . . ."[6] His work spans two literary periods—the end of the eighteenth and the first quarter of the nineteenth century. His writing includes examples of the genres and styles that prevailed during the Neoclassical and the Romantic periods. Tyler well repays the efforts of those who read his works. Royall Tyler deserves a significant place in the literary history of the United States.

Notes and References

The following abbreviations are used in the footnotes and bibliography entries.

MPT—Mary Palmer Tyler, *Grandmother Tyler's Book*.
PEL—Marius B. Péladeau.
RT—Royall Tyler.
TPT—Thomas Pickman Tyler, unpubl. "Memoir of Royall Tyler."
UVM—University of Vermont.
VHS—Vermont Historical Society.

Preface

1. John Quincy Adams, quoted in Randolph C. Randall, "Authors of *Port Folio* Revealed by the Hall Files," *American Literature*, XI (Jan. 1940), 380.
2. See Anon., "The Royall Tyler Collection," *Proceedings of the Vermont Historical Society*, N.S. IV:1 (1936), 3 - 4. Also see the agreement between the Tyler heirs and the VHS, *Vermont Historical Society News and Notes*, XV (July 1964), 84 - 86.
3. Katherine Schall Jarvis, "Royall Tyler's Lyrics for *May Day in Town*," *Harvard Library Bulletin*, XXIII:2 (Apr. 1975), 186 - 98.
4. Constance Rourke, *The Roots of American Culture and Other Essays*, ed. Van Wyck Brooks (Port Washington, N.Y., 1965), p. 124.

Chapter One

Where information can be found in more than one source, we have cited the source that is most readily available.

1. John S. Tyler to Thomas Pickman Tyler (June 6, 1872), unpubl. letter, VHS. All quotations from materials at the VHS are used with the kind permission of the Vermont Historical Society.
2. Thomas Pickman Tyler, unpubl. "Memoir of Royall Tyler," Part I, pp. 5 - 6. References are to the handwritten MS which is at the VHS. A typescript, erratically numbered, is also at the VHS.
3. John S. Tyler, unpubl. letter. Also see TPT, Pt. I, p. 2; and Intro. to RT, *The Algerine Captive*, ed. Don L. Cook (New Haven, 1970), p. 8.
4. John Langdon Sibley and Clifford K. Shipton, *Biographical Sketches of Those Who Attended Harvard College in the Classes 1741 - 1745* (1873; rpt. Boston, 1960), XI, 313.
5. *Ibid.*

6. Mary R. Cabot, *Annals of Brattleboro, 1681 - 1895* (Brattleboro, Vt., 1921), I, 251. Also see unpubl. letter from John S. Tyler, *op. cit.*

7. Sibley-Shipton, p. 313.

8. *Ibid.*, p. 317. Also see Lyman H. Butterfield, ed., *Diary and Autobiography of John Adams* (Cambridge, Mass., 1961), I, 392.

9. Thomas Hutchinson, *The History of Massachusetts Bay from 1749 to 1774. . .* , ed. Rev. John Hutchinson (New York, 1972), III, 191, 320. Also see Page Smith, *A New Age Now Begins* (New York, 1976), I, 344.

10. The King's Council was the twenty-eight-member upper house elected by the representatives. Cabot, p. 251; TPT, Pt. I, p. 5. Also see Walter Hill Crockett, *Vermont, the Green Mountain State* (New York, 1923), V, 71.

11. Helen Tyler Brown, "Introduction," in RT, *The Contrast,* ed. James Benjamin Wilbur (New York, 1970), p. xxv.

12. G. Thomas Tanselle, *Royall Tyler* (Cambridge, Mass., 1967), pp. 3, 222, n. 3.

13. On the typical college-preparatory studies of the time, see Robert Middlekauff, "A Persistent Tradition: The Classical Curriculum in Eighteenth-Century New England," *William and Mary Quarterly,* XVIII, series 3 (Jan. 1961), 62.

14. Sibley-Shipton, p. 318.

15. See John Langdon Sibley, apparently to Thomas Pickman Tyler (Nov. 25, 1873), unpubl. letter, VHS. For Harvard entrance requirements, see William Loring Andrews, compiler, *Prospect of the Colledges in Cambridge in New England* (New York, 1897), p. 5.

16. See Thomas Pickman Tyler, "Royall Tyler," *Vermont Bar Association, Act of Incorporation, Constitution, Members, and Papers and Addresses Read 1878 - 1881.* (Montpelier, Vt., 1882), p. 45. Also see *Catalogus Eorum qui in Collegio Harvardino . . .* (Boston, 1776), p. 32.

17. TPT, Pt. I, p. 15. John Langdon Sibley's unpubl. private journal (entry for Oct. 15, 1856) says that some knowledge about Harvard University was supplied to him by "Mr. Royall Morse, (illegitimate son of a woman who was a sweeper for very many years in the college buildings by a student, Royall Tyler)." Morse, born in June 1779, was a well-known Cambridge personage. No other reference to such a Tyler descendant exists. The quotation from Sibley can be found in L. H. Butterfield, Wendell D. Garrett, and Marc Friedlaender, "Introduction," *The Earliest Diary of John Adams* (Cambridge, Mass., 1966), p. 23.

18. TPT, Pt. I, p. 15.

19. Some commentators say that RT was valedictorian of his class; see Marius B. Péladeau, ed., *The Verse of Royall Tyler* (Charlottesville, Va., 1968), p. xv and xv, n. 5. An unpubl. letter to the authors of this book from Ms. Bonnie B. Salt, Assistant in the Harvard University Archives (June 26, 1975), states, "There were no commencement exercises for the public for the year 1776 due to the turbulent times and a small pox epidemic. . . . In

later years, the first scholar was determined by who gave a particular commencement part. . . . There is no way to determine who was the first scholar of the class." Also see *Catalogus Eorum qui* . . . , p. 32.

20. See unpubl. letter to Helen Tyler Brown from E. H. Tompkins (Jan. 30, 1918), Box 78, VHS, which says that "honorary B.A. degrees were given to men from other colleges upon request." Also see Bertrand William Chapman, *The Nativism of Royall Tyler* (unpubl. M.A. thesis, Univ. of Vermont, 1933), p. 3; and Butterfield, *Earliest Diary*, p. 22. An unpubl. letter to the authors of this book from Wesley H. Poling, Director of Alumni Records at Yale Univ. (Apr. 29, 1975), says, "Our best judgment is that the degree was awarded following a tradition of collegiate courtesy. . . ."

21. Massachusetts Secretary of Commonwealth, *Massachusetts Soldiers and Sailors of the Revolutionary War* (Boston, 1907), XVI, 240.

22. TPT, Pt. I, pp. 14 and 17; and Pt. IV, pp. 143 - 50. Apparently John Steele Tyler once offered to join the British, according to Lewis Einstein, *Divided Loyalties: Americans in England During the War of Independence* (London, 1933), pp. 365 - 66, 447, n. 14.

23. Cabot, I, 252.

24. Butterfield, *Earliest Diary*, p. 23, n. 50.

25. TPT, Pt. II, sec. 3, p. 39.

26. *Ibid.*, Pt. I, p. 18. Also see Cabot, I, 252 - 53.

27. TPT, Pt. I, pp. 20 - 21. Reference to Tyler's service is in the Tyler Papers, Box 77, Item 4, VHS. Also see "The Battle of Rhode Island" in Page Smith, *A New Age Now Begins*, II, 1106 - 22.

28. PEL, *Verse*, p. xvi.

29. William Willis, *History of Portland, from 1632 - 1864* . . . (Portland, Maine, 1865), pp. 625 - 26.

30. Inferior Court of Common Pleas, Suffolk, 1780, began and held at Boston with and for the Court of Suffolk; Tyler Papers, Box 78, VHS. Also see Tyler Papers (Aug. 19, 1780) Box 45, Item 20, VHS.

31. Samuel A. Bates, ed., *Records of the Town of Braintree* (Randolph, Mass., 1886), pp. 547, 549, 565 *et passim*.

32. TPT, Pt. I, sec. 2, p. 2.

33. L. H. Butterfield *et al.*, eds., *Adams Family Correspondence* (New York, 1965), IV, 335. Also see RT's comments on Lord Chesterfield in *The Contrast*.

34. Quoted in Butterfield, *Earliest Diary*, p. 18.

35. *Ibid.*, p. 21.

36. Quoted in Page Smith, *John Adams* (New York, 1962), I, 559.

37. *Ibid.*, p. 572.

38. Butterfield, *Earliest Diary*, p. 25.

39. *Ibid.*

40. *Ibid.*

41. Page Smith, *John Adams*, I, 591.

42. *Ibid.*

43. Unsigned letter (Apr. 3, 1784), Tyler Papers, MS. 18., VHS.

44. Butterfield, *Diary and Autobiography*, III, 156.

45. *Ibid.*, III, 160 - 61. Also see Page Smith, *John Adams*, I, 592 - 93.

46. Lida Mayo, "Miss Adams in Love," *American Heritage*, XVI (Feb. 1965), p. 39. Also on Smith see his daughter's book, *Journal and Correspondence of Miss Adams, Daughter of John Adams*, ed. Caroline Amelia [Smith] DeWindt (New York, 1841), pp. 7 - 96. The published version of Nabby's journal of her first year in Europe (1784) contains reports on social activities but no references to RT. A testimonial from George Washington helped William Smith get his position with the American legation. See DeWindt, p. 117.

47. Page Smith, *John Adams*, I, 559 - 60.

48. Mary Palmer Tyler, *Grandmother Tyler's Book*, eds. Frederick Tupper and Helen Tyler Brown (New York, 1925), p. 81.

49. See MPT, p. 77. Also see Katherine Metcalf Roof, *Colonel William Smith and Lady* (London, n.d.), p. 46.

50. Butterfield, *Earliest Diary*, p. 27.

51. Quoted in Butterfield, *Diary and Autobiography*, III, 192.

52. Quoted in Elizabeth Hunt Palmer, unpubl. memoir, [p. 9], Tyler Papers, VHS. See published version in MPT, p. 76.

53. Abigail Adams to Charles Storer (May 22, 1786), unpubl. letter, VHS.

54. Abigail Adams to Charles Storer (March 23, 1786), unpubl. letter, VHS.

55. Mayo, p. 89.

56. Page Smith, *John Adams*, II, 992.

57. See Butterfield, *Diary and Autobiography*, I, 217. In 1965, Wendell D. Garrett found at the VHS, in an unmarked manila folder, a MS that was determined to be a diary by John Adams, covering his third year at Harvard (1753 - 54). This work has been printed as *The Earliest Diary of John Adams*.

At one point, RT had borrowed some papers from Adams's library and commented to Mrs. Adams, ". . . you will I hope forgive the theft, when I deliver the paper to you. . ." (Butterfield, "Intro.," *Earliest Diary*, p. 19). No one knows why John Adams's diary was among RT's papers.

58. John S. Tyler to Thomas Pickman Tyler (June 15, 1872), unpubl. letter, VHS. Also see TPT, Pt. I, sec. 2, p. 11.

59. See Forrest McDonald and Ellen Shapiro McDonald, *Confederation and Constitution: 1781 - 1789* (Columbia, S.C., 1968), pp. 103 - 107; and Ray Allen Billington, Bert James Lowenberg, and Samuel High Brockunier, *The Making of American Democracy* (New York, 1957), I, 97 - 98. Also see Bruce Catton and William B. Catton, *The Bold and Magnificent Dream* (New York, 1978), pp. 326 - 28.

60. TPT, Pt. I, sec. 2, p. 14.

61. *Ibid.*, Pt. I, sec. 2, p. 16.

62. *Ibid.*, Pt. I, sec. 2, p. 19.
63. On Tyler's relationship with Ethan Allen, see PEL, "Royall Tyler and Ethan Allen's Appendix to *Reason the Only Oracle of Man*," *Vermont History*, XXXVI (Summer 1968), 155 - 58.
64. TPT, Pt. I, sec. 2, p. 47.
65. *Ibid.*, Pt. I, sec. 2, p. 43.
66. *Ibid.*, Pt. I, sec. 2, pp. 37 - 38.
67. From research by Frances A. Plimpton at the State House Archives Library in Boston, Mass., p. 2; in Tyler papers, Box 77, VHS.
68. Chronological Record, Plimpton research, VHS, p. 4. Also see Helen Tyler Brown, "Intro.," in Wilbur ed. of *Contrast*, p. xxviii.
69. Jarvis, pp. 186 - 98.
70. MPT, p. 107. Also see TPT, Pt. II, sec. 3, p. 26.
71. TPT, Pt. II, sec. 3, pp. 26 - 28.
72. On the Palmers see [Charles S. Palmer], "Biographical Sketch of General Joseph Palmer," *New Englander*, III (Jan. 1845), 1 - 23. Mary Palmer Tyler's nieces were the Peabody Sisters of Salem: Elizabeth Palmer Peabody, who in 1860 established the first kindergarten in America; Mary Palmer Peabody Mann, who married the educator Horace Mann; Sophia Amelia Hawthorne, who married the novelist Nathaniel Hawthorne. (See Louise Hall Tharp's *The Peabody Sisters of Salem*—Boston, 1950.) Mary Palmer Tyler's nephew was George Palmer Putnam, the publisher.
73. MPT, pp. 73 - 74.
74. *Ibid.*, p. 178.
75. *Ibid.*, pp. 178 - 79.
76. Crockett, *Vermont*, II, 50, 485. Also see Ray Bearse, ed., *Vermont/A Guide to the Green Mountain State* (Boston, 1968), p. 48. The population of Guilford decreased with every census after 1791 until 1960.
77. TPT, Pt. II, sec. 3, p. 35.
78. MPT, p. 204.
79. Broad Brook Grange #151, *Official History of Guilford, Vt.; 1678 - 1961* (Guilford, Vt., 1961), p. 110.
80. MPT, pp. 218, 227.
81. Cabot, I, 272.
82. James Elliot, "The Autumnal Seasons," in Cecil Hampden Howard, *Brattleborough in Verse and Prose* (Brattleborough, Vt., 1885), p. 131; also see Cabot, I, 213 - 14. In the nineteenth century, Rudyard Kipling received a far less favorable reception. See Philip Mason, *Kipling . . .* (New York, 1975), esp. pp. 123 - 25.
83. MPT, pp. 292 - 93.
84. Cabot, II, 834.
85. TPT, Pt. II, sec. 3, p. 36. Also see Milton Ellis, *Joseph Dennie and His Circle* (Austin, Tex., 1915). On RT and Dennie, see S. A. Bent, "Damon & Pythias Among Our Early Journalists," *New England Magazine*, N.S., XIX (Aug. 1896), 666 - 75.

86. See Andrew P. Peabody, "*The Farmer's Weekly Museum*," *Proceedings of the American Antiquarian Society*, N.S., VI (Oct. 1889), 106 - 29. Also see Frank Luther Mott, *American Journalism* . . . (New York, 1950), p. 159.

87. TPT, Pt. III, sec. 5, p. 23.

88. J[ohn] A. Graham, *A Descriptive Sketch of the Present State of Vermont, one of the United States of America* (London, 1797), pp. 154 - 55.

89. See Lillie D. Loshe, *The Early American Novel* (New York, 1907), p. 109, and Tanselle, *Royall Tyler*, p. 145. Also see Tanselle, "Early American Fiction in England: The Case of *The Algerine Captive*," *Papers of the Bibliographical Society of America*, LIX (Oct. 1965), 367 - 84.

90. Arthur Hobson Quinn, *A History of American Drama from the Beginning to the Civil War* (New York, 1946), pp. 71, 449. Also see PEL, "Royall Tyler's *Other* Plays," *New England Quarterly*, 40 (Mar. 1967), pp. 56 - 57.

91. See *The Prose of Royall Tyler*, ed. Marius B. Péladeau (Montpelier and Rutland, Vt., 1972), pp. 269 - 80.

92. Mary Palmer Tyler (Feb. 14, 1800), unpubl. letter, Box 50, VHS.

93. The Tyler children were as follows: Royall, Jr. (1794 - 1813), died while a student at the university in Burlington, Vermont. John Steele Tyler (1796 - 1876) was a merchant in Boston. Mary Whitwell Tyler (1798 - 1874) was a kindergarten teacher. Edward Royall Tyler (1800 - 1848) was a Congregational minister and editor of the *New Englander*. William Clark Tyler (1802 - 1882) was a merchant in Boston. Joseph Dennie Tyler (1804 - 1852) was an Episcopal minister and principal of the Asylum for Deaf Mutes in Virginia. Amelia Sophia Tyler (1807 - 1878) was called "Teacher of 3 Generations." George Palmer Tyler, D.D. (1809 - 1896) was a Congregational and Presbyterian minister. Charles Tyler (1812 - 1896), who changed his name to Royall, became a Vermont lawyer and judge. Thomas Pickman Tyler, D.D. (1815 - 1892) was an Episcopal minister. His lengthy but unfinished biography of RT is a valuable study of an American writer, his life and times. Abiel Winship Tyler (1818 - 1832) died in his early teens. Consult MPT chronology, Appendix A, pp. 331, 333. Also see Tyler family Bible, VHS.

94. MPT, p. 270.

95. Martha V. Smith, "On Meeting House Hill," *Vermonter*, 26 (1927), 22 - 25.

96. For information on RT and the Vermont Supreme Court, see TPT, Pt. III, sec. 6, pp. 31 and 32; Pt. III, sec. 7, pp. 1, 2, 3, 4 *et passim*. Also see Frederick Tupper, "Royall Tyler," *Proceedings of the Vermont Historical Society*, Vol. 4 (1926 - 1927 - 1928), 65 - 101. Also consult G. R. Minot, ed., *Records of the Governor and Council of the State of Vermont*, Vol. 4 (1791 - 1804), 253, 337, 373 *et passim;* Vol. 5 (1804 - 1812), 12, 71, 108, 155, 192, 205, 286, 353 *et passim;* Vol. 6 (1813 - 1821), 16, 25 (Montpelier, Vt., 1876, 1877, 1878).

97. See PEL, "Royall Tyler and the University of Vermont," *Vermont History,* 42, No. 1 (Winter 1974), pp. 25, 29. RT's original draft of "the laws of the university" are in an unpubl. MS at the Univ. of Vermont, 19 unnumbered pages. Working on the MS with RT was William C. Bradley.

98. On RT and the UVM, see PEL, "Royall Tyler and the University." Also see President D. C. Sanders of UVM to RT (Dec. 5, 1810), unpubl. letter, Special Collections, UVM. Also see Crockett, V, 74, and Julian Ira Lindsey, *Tradition Looks Forward: The University of Vermont: A History, 1791 - 1904* (Burlington, Vt., 1904), pp. 15 *et passim.* An unpubl., undated memorandum by former UVM Registrar F. W. Kehoe provides a chronology on "The connection of the Hon. Royall Tyler with the Corporation of the University of Vermont," Box 77, VHS. On RT as Professor of Jurisprudence, T. D. Seymour Bassett, UVM Archivist, in an unpubl. letter to the authors of this book (May 2, 1975), states, "There have been no other members of the UVM faculty appointed to teach jurisprudence except medical jurisprudence . . . taught by a usually elderly member of the local bar, 1853 - date, in a few lectures. . . . [Péladeau's article] produces no evidence that Tyler actually taught jurisprudence. . . . So I would call Tyler a titular Professor of Jurisprudence."

99. Walpole, N.H.: Printed for Thomas & Thomas by D. & T. Carlisle, 1801.

100. On RT and Riley, see TPT, Pt. I, sec. 7, pp. 3 - 4, and Pt. IV, pp. 80 - 82, 282.

101. M. D. Gilman, *The Bibliography of Vermont* (Burlington, Vt., 1897), p. 282.

102. For an example of RT's apparent change of political sentiment, see TPT, Pt. IV, p. 32; also see Pt. III, sec. 7, p. 43. For an explanation of political shifts at that time, see Samuel Eliot Morison and Henry Steele Commager, *The Growth of the American Republic* (New York, 1960), I, 351 - 54.

103. For the correspondence see TPT, Pt. III, sec. 8, pp. 16 - 19, 19 - 24, 25; Pt. IV, pp. 1 - 3, 4 - 6, 6 - 12, 16 - 20 *et passim.*

104. RT to James Fisk (May 13, 1812), unpubl. letter in TPT, Pt. IV, pp. 166 - 72, esp. p. 169. Also see Roger H. Brown, "A Vermont Republican Urges War: Royall Tyler, 1912, and the Subject of Republican Government," *Vermont History,* 36, No. 1 (Winter 1968), 13 - 18.

105. See Crockett, *Vermont,* V, 74; also Minot, V and VI.

106. See the pathetic unpubl. letter from RT to his son John Steele Tyler (Nov. 7, 1813), VHS.

107. MPT, pp. 323 - 24.

108. RT mentions his predicament to Mary in an unpubl. letter VHS, Box 45. The letter has a penned note "Ca. 1812," but the contents apparently refer to the period after RT left the court in Oct. 1813.

109. Prentiss C. Dodge, ed., *Encyclopedia of Vermont Biography* (Burlington, Vt., 1912), p. 82.

110. Mary Palmer Tyler, entry for June 10, 1822, unpubl. diary, VHS, n. pag.

111. RT worked on "Utile Dulci" as late as April 16, 1825. See Mary Palmer Tyler, unpubl. diary.

112. See Mary Palmer Tyler to Amelia Sophia Tyler (Jan. 19, 1825), unpubl. letter, VHS.

113. "The Chestnut Tree" was printed in a pamphlet ed. for the Driftwind Press by Walter John Coates (North Montpelier, Vt., 1931); also see PEL, *Verse*, pp. 194 - 216.

114. PEL, *Prose*, pp. 37 - 174.

115. Unpubl. letter, VHS.

116. Mary Palmer Tyler, unpubl. diary, VHS.

117. *Ibid.*

118. MPT, pp. 74 - 75.

Chapter Two

1. Wilbur ed., p. vii.

2. TPT, Pt. I, sec. 3, p. 1.

3. See A. H. Quinn, *American Drama*, p. 32.

4. For the plays performed during Tyler's visit to New York, see George O. Seilhamer, *History of the American Theatre*, II (Philadelphia, 1889), 214 - 15.

5. Thomas J. McKee, "Introduction," in the Dunlap Society's edition of RT's *The Contrast* (New York, 1887), p. vi.

6. For example, *The Provoked Husband* by Sir John Vanbrugh (completed by Colley Cibber, 1728) was "read" in Boston in 1770. See A. H. Nethercot, "Dramatic Background of Royall Tyler's *The Contrast*," *American Literature*, XII (Jan. 1941), 438.

7. See Ch. XII (pp. 141 - 49) and Ch. XV (esp. pp. 168 - 69) in PEL, *Prose*.

8. Brown in Wilbur ed., p. xxviii.

9. Candour, New York *Daily Advertiser*, April 18, 1787; rpt. in Montrose J. Moses and John Mason Brown, *American Theatre As Seen by Its Critics, 1752 - 1934* (New York, 1934), pp. 24 - 25.

10. Wilbur ed., p. 20. Hereafter, all quotations from *The Contrast* refer to the AMS Press edition of RT's *The Contrast*, ed. James Benjamin Wilbur (New York, 1970). Quotations from the Wilbur edition are used with the kind permission of AMS Press. The original edition of *The Contrast* (Philadelphia, 1790) indicates that certain lines were omitted in the stage production. For an indication of these omissions, see Arthur Hobson Quinn, *Representative American Plays* (New York, 1938), pp. 47 - 77, esp. p. 50.

11. Seilhamer, however, says the prologue is "not from Major Tyler's pen," II, 227. The ideas in the prologue are similar to sentiments expressed elsewhere by RT. See the preface to *Captive*, pp. 27 - 29; and "Introduction to the Sacred Dramas," in PEL, *Prose*, p. 443. The theme of en-

couraging native American literature is discussed in R. W. B. Lewis, *The American Adam* (Chicago, 1955), esp. pp. 1 - 5, 77. Lewis's discussion, however, emphasizes the nineteenth century. The remarks in *The Contrast* are earlier.

12. Seilhamer, II, 214.

13. RT expresses disapproval of dueling in several works. For example, see Vol. I, ch. 12, of *Captive;* and "The Runner, or Indian Talk" (*Newhampshire and Vermont Journal*, Aug. 9, 1796), rpt. in PEL, *Prose*, p. 211.

14. Allan Gates Halline, *American Plays* (New York, 1935), p. 5. Also see Roger B. Stein, "Royall Tyler and the Question of Our Speech," *New England Quarterly*, XXXVIII (Dec. 1965), 454 - 74. Oliver Wendell Holmes called Emerson's "American Scholar" (1837) this nation's "intellectual Declaration of Independence."

15. See RT's description of an American fop abroad in *The Yankey in London* (New York, 1809), Letter LXIV, pp. 167 - 70. Also see Kent G. Gallagher, *The Foreigner in Early American Drama* (The Hague, 1966), p. 36.

16. See RT's "Oration on the Death of Washington," in PEL, *Prose*, pp. 272 - 80, and the poem "An Occasional Address," in PEL, *Verse*, p. 43. Also see *The Island of Barrataria*, ed. Arthur Wallace Peach and George Floyd Newbrough, in *Four Plays by Royall Tyler*, vol. 15 bound with vol. 16 of *America's Lost Plays*, ed. Barrett H. Clark (Bloomington, Ind., 1965), 17.

17. Cf. the sentimental Maria in Richard Brinsley Sheridan's *School for Scandal.* Manly, despite his honor, occasionally sounds like the sanctimonious Joseph Surface of Sheridan's play. The misanthropic hero of William Wycherly's *Plain Dealer* (1676) is also named Manly, as is the sentimental and righteous hero in *The Provoked Husband.* See n. 6 above.

18. Anon., *Worcester Magazine* (Worcester, Mass.), III (May 1787), p. 61.

19. Anon., *The Maryland Gazette or, the Baltimore Advertiser* (Nov. 13, 1787), p. 3.

20. Perley Isaac Reed, *The Realistic Presentation of American Characters in Native Plays Prior to Eighteen Seventy*, in *Ohio State University Bulletin*, XXII, No. 26 (May 1918), p. 50.

21. Seilhamer, II, 226.

22. Stein, p. 457.

23. Chapman, p. 11.

24. See R. W. B. Lewis, p. 5.

25. The "purling streams" is a reference to the Della Cruscan style which RT satirized in *The Yankey in London*, pp. 12 - 13, and in such poems as "Address to Della Crusca," in PEL, *Verse*, pp. 59 - 61. Tyler's Della Cruscan satires are discussed in our Ch. 6 and 7.

26. Mary Palmer Tyler approvingly quotes Maria's words in an unpubl. letter to Elizabeth Hunt Palmer (Feb. 14, 1800), Box 50, VHS.

27. In Act I, sc. II, of Richard Brinsley Sheridan's *The Rivals*, Lydia

Languish refers to a suitor, Bob Acres, as the "odious Acres. . . ." Tyler's attitude toward Anglicized Americans was expressed in the mid-1780s, when he complimented John Quincy Adams for displaying "no tincture of what we style European frivolity of manners." Quoted in Page Smith, *John Adams*, II, 661.

28. Stein, p. 465.

29. Quoted in Butterfield, *Earliest Diary*, p. 29.

30. See Reed, p. 53.

31. *Tears and Smiles* also imitates RT's rustic Jonathan in the rural comic character of Nathan Yank.

32. See Stein, p. 464. Also see John Lauber, "*The Contrast:* A Study in the Concept of Innocence," *English Language Notes*, I (Sept. 1963), pp. 33 - 37.

33. See Mr. Tiffany, "A New York Merchant," in Anna Cora Mowatt Ritchie's *Fashion* (1845). This successful play liberally imitates Tyler's *Contrast*. Mrs. Mowatt's drama features an officer, Col. Howard, and a comic rustic, Adam Trueman. Charles E. Lown, Jr., calls Van Rough a "prototype . . . of the businessman character." See "The Businessman in Early American Drama," *Educational Theatre Journal*, XV (Mar. 1963), p. 48.

34. Stein, p. 468. Tyler described Franklin several times, as in Vol. I, ch. 23, of *Captive*.

35. "Impartial Review," *Universal Asylum and Columbian Magazine* (Philadelphia), V (July 1790), 118.

36. See Alton Ketchum, *Uncle Sam: The Man and the Legend* (New York, 1959), p. 28. On the origins of Brother Jonathan, see Albert Matthews, "Brother Jonathan," *Publications of the Colonial Society of Massachusetts*, VII (1900 - 1902), 94 - 122; and Matthews, "Brother Jonathan Once More," *Publications of the Colonial Society of Massachusetts*, XXXII (1936), 374 - 86. Matthews also discusses the Yankee symbols in "Uncle Sam," *Proceedings of the American Antiquarian Society*, N.S. XIX (1908 - 1909), 21 - 65. On "Yankee Doodle" see Oscar George Theodore Sonnek, *Report on "The Star Spangled Banner"/"Hail Columbia"/"America"/"Yankee Doodle"* (Washington, 1909), esp. pp. 79 - 164. Also see Grenville Vernon, *Yankee Doodle-Doo* (New York, 1927), pp. 23 - 24.

37. See R. W. G. Vail, "*Adventures of Jonathan Corncob, Loyal American Refugee* (1787)/A Commentary," *Papers of the Bibliographical Society of America*, 50 (1956), 101 - 14. Also see *Adventures of Jonathan Corncob*, ed. Noel Perrin (Boston, 1976).

38. On the discovery of Atkinson's play and its Jonathen, see Marston Balch, "Jonathan the First," *Modern Language Notes*, XLVI:5 (May 1931), 281 - 88. Also see Matthews, "Brother Jonathan Once More," pp. 384 - 86.

39. Balch, p. 287. Halline agrees, p. 7.

40. Anon. review, *Maryland Gazette* (Nov. 13, 1787), p. 3.

41. William Dunlap, *History of the American Theater* (1832; rpt. New York, 1963), p. 137. Lauber also sees Jonathan as a clown, p. 37. Dunlap's

play *The Modest Soldier* (*c.* 1788), no longer extant, was a conscious imitation of *The Contrast.* See Dunlap, *History*, p. 147.

42. Dunlap, *History*, p. 162.

43. Reed, p. 13.

44. Jonathan W. Curvin, "The Stage Yankee," in *Studies in Speech and Drama in Honor of Alexander M. Drummond* (Ithaca, N.Y., 1944), p. 129.

45. Rourke, *Roots*, p. 120.

46. The term "malapropism" refers to a comic error, an inappropriate use of a word. The device is associated with the comic Mrs. Malaprop, who appeared in Richard Brinsley Sheridan's *The Rivals* (1775).

47. Andrew Barton's *Disappointment* used the tune of "Yankee Doodle" with original words. The play was scheduled for production in 1767 but was withdrawn. Barton is apparently a pseudonym for Thomas Forrest. In place of *The Disappointment,* Thomas Godfrey's *Prince of Parthia* was produced, thus gaining the honor of being the first American play to be professionally produced. See A. H. Quinn, *American Drama,* pp. 16, 29.

48. Balch, p. 287.

49. Paul Bruce Pettit, "The Important American Dramatic Types to 1900," Diss., Cornell, 1949, p. 97. Also see George H. McKnight and Bert Emsley, *The Evolution of the English Language from Chaucer to the Twentieth Century* (New York, 1956), p. 480.

50. Accounts of the stage Yankee appear in numerous works. See especially: Curvin, pp. 139 - 42; Richard M. Dorson, "The Yankee on Stage—a Folk Hero of American Drama," *New England Quarterly,* XIII (Sept. 1940), 467 - 93; Louis M. Eich, "The Stage Yankee," *Quarterly Journal of Speech,* XXVII (Feb. 1941), 16 - 25; Francis Hodge, *Yankee Theatre: The Image of America on the Stage, 1825 - 1850* (Austin, Tex., 1964); James Joseph Quinn, "The Jonathan Character in the American Drama," Diss., Columbia, 1955; Lawrence P. Spingarn, "The Yankee in Early American Fiction," *New England Quarterly,* XXXI (Sept. 1958), pp. 484 - 95; Robert C. Toll, *On With the Show* (New York, 1976), pp. 10 - 13. See also John Perry, *James A. Herne* (Chicago, 1978), for discussions of rustic characters.

51. Dorson, p. 468.

52. See Candour's critique of the song, rpt. in Moses and Brown, p. 24.

53. See Rourke, *Roots,* pp. 69 - 70. See also Walt Whitman's poem "Osceola," in *Leaves of Grass,* 1891 ed. The concept of the Noble Savage was popular in the eighteenth century. See Alexander Pope's comments on the "Poor Indian" in "Essay on Man" (1733) and Jean-Jacques Rousseau's "Discourse on the Origin of Inequality" (1750).

54. Frank Edgar Farley, "The Dying Indian," in *Anniversary Papers by Colleagues and Pupils of George Lyman Kittredge* (New York, 1967), p. 252. The music to "Alknomook" is reprinted in the McKee ed. of *Contrast,* p. 10.

55. See G. Thomas Tanselle, review of *Verse of Royall Tyler*, ed. Marius B. Péladeau, *American Literature,* XLI, No. 1 (Mar. 1969), 119.

56. On this magazine see Frank Luther Mott, *History of American Magazines, 1741 - 1850* (Cambridge, Mass., 1957), p. 100.

57. See Farley's discussion of the printing history, p. 253. Also see PEL, *Verse*, p. 9, n. 1; McKee ed. of *Contrast*, p. x; Wilbur ed. of *Contrast*, pp. xxxii - xxxv.

58. Fred Lewis Pattee, *The Poems of Philip Freneau* (New York, 1963), II, 313. Pattee reprints Alknomook as "The Death Song of a Cherokee Indian," with several changes; see II, 313 - 14. The Alknomook poem, without the second stanza, also appeared in John Scawen's *New Spain, or Love in Mexico* (1790), an English opera. In 1806 Mrs. Anne Hunter in her *Poems* claimed Alknomook as her own. In 1821 Maria Edgeworth, the Irish novelist, used the poem in her novel *Rosamond*, crediting it to Mrs. Hunter. See Farley, p. 253.

59. Unpubl. letter of March 20, 1918; also see unpubl. letters of March 13, 1918, and March 23, 1918; VHS. A similar reference to RT's authorship occurs in A. H. Quinn's *History of American Drama* (2nd ed., 1943), p. 71.

60. McKee ed. of *Contrast*, p. x.

61. Candour, rpt. in Moses and Brown, p. 24.

62. On the play as being "talky," see George C. D. Odell, *Annals of the American Stage, 1699 - 1894* (New York, 1927), I, 256.

63. Stein, p. 460.

64. Quinn, *American Drama*, pp. 5, 16 - 17.

65. Robert Rogers's unproduced *Ponteach* (pub. 1766) is the earliest American play on an American theme. See Quinn, *American Drama*, pp. 28 - 29.

66. Hancock and the fire at Boston are cited in the Wilbur ed. of *Contrast*, p. xxx. For the performance during Washington's inauguration, see MPT, pp. 118 - 19. Other discussions of the play's stage history can be found in: William Bishop, "First American Comedy: *The Contrast*," *Mentor*, 15 (Jan. 1928), 39; Joseph Ireland, *Records of the New York Stage* (New York, 1866), I, 76, 80; A. H. Quinn, *American Drama*, p. 65; Odell, pp. 255, 274; Seilhamer, II (1888), 222, 234, 238, 246 and III (1889), 11, 207, 211, 245. However, Tanselle, *Royall Tyler*, pp. 51, 243, n. 7; and Wilbur, *Contrast*, p. xxx, list only four productions during the 1787 season. Mary Palmer Tyler says *The Contrast* "was written and had a wonderful run" in the winter of 1788 - 89; see MPT, p. 107. RT's son Thomas Pickman Tyler says that *The Contrast* was first produced at the Park Street Theatre in the Spring of 1789 "and had an unprecedented run of several weeks." TPT, Pt. I, sec. 3, p. 6. To add to the confusion, Evert A. and George L. Duyckinck's *Cyclopaedia of American Literature* (Philadelphia, 1855), an influential nineteenth-century reference work, gives the date of production of *The Contrast* as 1786; see I, 432. Similarly the influential twentieth-century critic F. O. Matthiessen uses the year of 1786 in *American Renaissance* (1941; rpt. London, 1970), p. 200.

67. Tanselle, *Royall Tyler*, p. 52.

68. *Independent Chronical and Universal Advertiser* (Oct. 18, 1792), quoted in Quinn, *American Drama,* p. 65.

69. Quinn, *American Drama,* p. 65; Seilhamer, II, 215.

70. On these productions see Doc. Boxes 47 and 50, VHS; miscellaneous letters, MSS.9, VHS; and Wilbur ed., p. 117.

71. Burns Mantle, *The Best Plays of 1933 - 1940* (New York, 1960), p. 457.

72. John and Mollie G. Gassner, *Best Plays of the Early American Theater* (New York, 1967), p. xxviii.

73. Otis L. Guernsey, *The Best Plays of 1971 - 1972* (New York, 1972), p. 380.

74. The opening ceremonies at the University of Vermont also included a readers' theater production of RT's *Judgement of Solomon* (March 20 and 21, 1974). The director of the Hamline University production of *Contrast,* William H. Kimes, wrote to us (unpubl. letter, June 9, 1976), "Audiences seemed to respond very favorably to the production. . . . We were somewhat pleasantly surprised to see just *how* well the script played. It came across as a solid comedy which justified itself in stage terms. . . ." On the East Hampton production, see Mel Gussow, "Early Americana in Hamptons," *New York Times* (July 16, 1976), sec. C, p. 4. On the GeVa performances, see Maury Klein, "Life Upon the Wicked Stage," *American History Illustrated,* XI, No. 10 (Feb. 1977), 43. Klein implies fewer productions of *The Contrast* than actually took place.

75. *Maryland Journal and Baltimore Advertiser* (Nov. 27, 1787), p. 10.

76. The list of subscribers is reprinted in the Wilbur ed., pp. 7 - 19. Also see Paul Leicester Ford, *Washington and the Theater* (1899; rpt. New York, 1967), p. 44. Apparently Washington never attended a performance of *The Contrast.*

77. Wilbur ed., pp. vii - xiii. Also see L. E. Chittenden, *Personal Reminiscences (1840 - 90)* (New York, 1893).

78. George Washington's autographed copy is now in the Special Collections of the UVM Library. A second copy was found only a few weeks after Chittenden's discovery. This second copy was purchased by Thomas J. McKee.

79. See G. Thomas Tanselle, "Some Uncollected Authors XLII/Royall Tyler, 1757 - 1826," *Book Collector,* XV (Autumn 1966), 303 - 20. Tanselle lists twelve copies (p. 310). There is also an unbound copy at the Clements Library of the Univ. of Michigan.

80. Candour, rpt. in Moses and Brown, pp. 24 - 25.

81. Philo Dramaticus, cited in miscellaneous unpubl. letters, VHS.

82. *Maryland Gazette,* p. 3. Seilhamer, II, 233, quotes a review from the *Pennsylvania Herald* (Nov. 13, 1787), which is apparently the same as the *Maryland Gazette* review. See MSS.9, VHS.

83. *Maryland Journal,* p. 3.

84. *Worcester Magazine,* p. 61.

85. *Massachusetts Magazine,* VI (Mar. 1794), pp. 179 - 80. See G. Thomas Tanselle, "Royall Tyler, Judith Sargent Murray, and *The Medium,*" *New England Quarterly,* XLI (Mar. 1968), 115 - 17.

86. Dunlap, *History,* p. 137. "Dunlap may be jealous of Tyler's work, the first native play to be professionally produced after the revolution, thus cheating Dunlap of a certain place in history." This analysis appears in Robert H. Canary, *William Dunlap* (New York, 1970), p. 58.

87. Seilhamer, II, 231.

88. Nethercot, p. 436.

89. Montrose J. Moses, "American Plays of Our Forefathers," *North American Review,* 215:6 (June 1922), p. 797.

90. A. H. Quinn, *American Drama,* p. 66.

91. Rourke, *Roots,* p. 119.

92. Van Wyck Brooks, *The World of Washington Irving* (Philadelphia, 1945), p. 160.

93. In Walter Blair, Theodore Hornberger, Randall Stewart, eds., *The Literature of the United States* (Chicago, 1953), I, 423.

94. "Stage: 1787's 'The Contrast' Returns with Spirit," *New York Times* (Nov. 28, 1972), p. 51.

95. Review in *Nation* (Dec. 18, 1972), p. 637.

96. "Why Do They Speak?" *New York Times* (Dec. 24, 1972), sec. II, p. 7.

Chapter Three

1. Seilhamer, II, 215.

2. MPT, p. 107.

3. William Grayson to James Madison (May 24, 1787), quoted in Worthington C. Ford, "Federal Constitution of Virginia 1787 - 1788," *Proceedings of the Massachusetts Historical Society,* 2nd Series, XVII (1903), 461.

4. Seilhamer, II, 215 - 16.

5. For the use of such techniques, see Oscar George Theodore Sonnek, *Early Opera in America* (New York, 1963), p. 79.

6. Jarvis, p. 186; see above Ch. 1, n. 69. Hereafter, all quotations from *May Day* are taken from the pamphlet rpt. in Ms. Jarvis's article. Quotations are used with the kind permission of Ms. Jarvis and the President and Fellows of Harvard College.

7. A comic black character, Raccoon, is included in an unproduced play *Disappointment* by Andrew Barton (pseudonym for Thomas Forrest); see above Ch. 2, n. 47. Isaac Bickerstaffe's *The Padlock* (London, 1768; New York, 1769) is an English comic opera featuring a black character, Mungo. See Allardyce Nicoll, *History of English Drama,* III (Cambridge, Eng., 1927), 237. Ms. Jarvis notes (p. 190) that Lewis Hallam, who played Mungo, also played Pompey in *May Day.* See also Ralpho in Robert Munford's *The Candidates* (pre-1776?), mentioned in A. H. Quinn, *History of American Drama,* pp. 54 - 55, 124.

8. Seilhamer, III, 247 - 48.

9. See A. H. Quinn, *History of American Drama,* pp. 126, 459; and Tanselle, "Royall Tyler, Judith Sargent Murray, and *The Medium,*" p. 115.

10. PEL, "Royall Tyler's *Other* Plays," p. 54. RT's oldest son, Royall, Jr., wrote an unpubl. adaptation of Moliere's *Doctor in Spite of Himself* entitled *The Dumb Gent.* It was produced at the UVM in 1812 and again at the UVM on March 20 and 21, 1974. Lindsay's history of the UVM refers to Royall, Jr.'s play as "Quackery"; see pp. 102 - 103. Also see the letter dated Oct. 7, 1795 (New Hampshire Historical Society), in the Tyler-Dennie correspondence for a mention of Tyler's *The Mock Doctor.*

11. See Nicoll, p. 278. Kemble's play opened at Drury Lane, London, in 1789 and in New York in 1795.

12. "Chief Justice Royall Tyler," [*Brattleboro Correspondence Sunday Republican,* 1892, n. pag.], courtesy Brattleboro, Vt., Public Library.

13. See Wilbur ed., p. 118.

14. Quoted in A. H. Quinn, "Royall Tyler," *Dictionary of American Biography,* XIX (1936), p. 96. Also see TPT, Pt. II, sec. 4, pp. 1 - 2.

15. See TPT, Pt. II, sec. 4, p. 2.

16. PEL, "Royall Tyler's *Other* Plays," p. 57.

17. *Columbian Centinel,* XXVIII, No. 16 (Oct. 28, 1797), [p. 4]. Royall Tyler, Jr., wrote an unpubl. and unproduced play entitled *The Speculators.* The MS, graciously supplied to us by Mrs. Dorothy Sutherland Melville, bears no relationship to the Yazoo land scandals.

18. See Miguel de Cervantes, *Don Quixote,* Ozell's revision of the translation of Peter Motteux (New York, 1930), pp. 716 - 803.

19. Tyler, *The Island of Barrataria,* in *Four Plays by Royall Tyler,* p. 1. Hereafter, all quotations from this play refer to *The Island of Barrataria,* ed. Arthur Wallace Peach and George Floyd Newbrough, in *Four Plays by Royall Tyler,* vol. 15 bound with vol. 16 of *America's Lost Plays,* ed. Barrett H. Clark (Bloomington, Ind., 1965). Quotations are used with the kind permission of Princeton University Press and Indiana University Press.

20. See Nicoll, p. 298; and the cast list for D'Urfey's *Barrataria* in Seilhamer, II, 259.

21. See MSS 559, VHS.

22. Mary Palmer Tyler to Amelia Tyler (Jan. 19, 1825), unpubl. letter, VHS. Also see Tyler's "Introduction to the Sacred Dramas" in PEL, *Prose,* p. 443.

23. Hereafter, all quotations from *Joseph and His Brethren* refer to the Peach-Newbrough edition of *Four Plays. . . .*

24. Mary Palmer Tyler to Amelia Tyler (Jan. 19, 1825).

25. *Ibid.*

26. Hereafter, all quotations from *The Judgement of Solomon* refer to the Peach-Newbrough edition of *Four Plays. . . .*

27. Carl William Engelhart, "An Historical and Critical Study of Royall Tyler," unpubl. M.A. thesis, Univ. of Minnesota, 1943, p. 55.

28. Mary Palmer Tyler to Amelia Tyler (Jan. 19, 1825).

29. RT Collection, VHS; rpt. in PEL, *Prose,* p. 443.

30. *Ibid.* Tyler uses the term "homespun" several times in relation to writing. Cf. Anne Bradstreet's "The Author to Her Book" (1678). Tyler refers to Mrs. Bradstreet's poetry in *The Bay Boy*, PEL, *Prose*, p. 52.

31. Hereafter all quotations from *The Origin of the Feast of Purim* refer to the Peach-Newbrough edition of *Four Plays. . . .* In *Purim*, Haman's wife is called Geresh; in the Book of Esther, she is called Zeresh. See Tanselle, *Royall Tyler*, p. 255, n. 29.

32. The tone here is similar to Orsino's opening lines in Shakespeare's *Twelfth Night*, "If music be the food of love, play on. . . ."

33. A. H. Quinn, *American Drama*, p. 72.

34. Unpubl. diary, VHS, n. pag.

35. See PEL, *Prose*, pp. 462 - 67; "Pumpkins" is discussed briefly in our Ch. 6.

36. PEL, *Verse*, pp. 221 - 24.

Chapter Four

1. *Massachusetts Spy*, Oct. 25, 1797, quoted in Chapman, p. 22.

2. MPT, pp. 258 - 59.

3. See Don L. Cook's intro. to his ed. of *Captive* for a brief but useful discussion of RT's possible sources, esp. pp. 18, 159*n*, and 161*n*. Also see Chapman, pp. 24 - 26, and Engelhart, p. 68.

4. Edward Royall Tyler, letter to Francis Joy Underhill (Apr. 6, 1926), quoted in Josephine C. Frost, *Underhill Genealogy* (Boston, 1932), II, 50.

5. See Richard Vanderbeets, "The Indian Captivity Narrative as Ritual," *American Literature*, XLIII:4 (Jan. 1972), 548 - 62.

6. MPT, pp. 228 - 29.

7. On editions of *Captive*, see Tanselle, "Some Uncollected Authors," p. 312, and Cook ed. of *Captive*, p. 24. On the publication in England see G. Thomas Tanselle, "Early American Fiction in England: The Case of *The Algerine Captive*," *Papers of the Bibliographical Society of America*, LIX (Oct. 1965), 367 - 84. On Tyler's place in the development of the American novel see the listing in Loshe, pp. 106 - 20. Also see Oscar Wegelin, *Early American Fiction: 1774 - 1830* (New York, 1929).

8. See John Shippen, "Character and Effects of Modern Novels" (1792), quoted in Rex J. Burbank and Jack B. Moore, *The Literature of Early America* (Columbus, O., 1967), p. 574. Also see the Scholars' Facsimiles and Reprints ed. of *Captive*, intro. Jack B. Moore (Gainesville, Fla., 1967), pp. vii - viii.

9. See title page in the Cook ed. of *Captive*, p. 25. Hereafter, all quotations from *Captive* refer to the Cook edition. Quotations are used with the kind permission of College and University Press.

10. Cook, p. 26.

11. Moore, p. viii.

12. For a discussion of the effects of genealogical openings in novels, see Huntington Brown, *Prose Styles* (Minneapolis, 1966), pp. 122 - 23. For a

discussion of the thematic relationship of the Captain Underhill section to the rest of the novel, see William C. Spengemann, *The Adventurous Muse: The Poetics of American Fiction, 1789 - 1900* (New Haven, 1977), p. 125.

13. L. W. Lawrence to Helen Tyler Brown, unpubl. letter (postmarked Jan. 29, 1918), VHS#59.

14. The use of classical declamation as a source of humor also occurs in Henry Fielding's *Joseph Andrews* (1742), Bk. II, Chs. II, III, V. Updike combines traits found in Joseph and in Parson Adams.

15. MPT, p. 96; also see TPT, Pt. II, sec. 3, pp. 4 - 5.

16. Tyler refers to quackery in *Barrataria.* See our Ch. 6 for Tyler's remarks on quackery in the John Johnson case. Also see TPT, Pt. III, sec. 8, pp. 1 - 4, and PEL, *Prose,* pp. 406 - 407. The MS of TPT appears to spell the quack's name as "John Johnstone."

17. William Dunlap, *Diary (1766 - 1839)* (New York, 1969), I, 174.

18. See Morison and Commager, pp. 388 - 89.

19. On such labor, see L. G. Barnby, *Prisoners of Algiers* (London, 1966), pp. 43, 55.

20. See Ada Lou Carson and Herbert L. Carson, "Royall Tyler and America's Divided Mind," *American Jewish Archives,* XXVIII (Apr. 1976), 79 - 84. Also see Barnby, esp. p. 84.

21. The last words of *Captive* are borrowed from John Dickinson's "Liberty Song" (1768): "By uniting we stand, by dividing we fall." The lines also appear in a fable, "The Four Oxen and the Lion," by Aesop. Also see Robert S. Forsythe, "'*The Algerine Captive,*' 1802," *Notes and Queries,* CLXXII (May 29, 1937), 389 - 90.

22. Updike, like Colonel Manly, has some of the traits of an American Adam. See R. W. B. Lewis, p. 5.

23. See Larry R. Dennis, "Legitimizing the Novel: Royall Tyler's *The Algerine Captive,*" *Early American Literature,* IX, No. 1 (Spring 1974), 73.

24. TPT, Pt. II, sec. 4, p. 18.

25. "SELECTMEN of Windsor *against* STEPHEN JACOB, Esquire," rpt. in PEL, *Prose,* p. 393.

26. "Retrospective Review," *Monthly Anthology and Boston Review,* IX (Nov. 1810), 346.

27. For possible sources, see Chapman, p. 26; Engelhart, p. 68; and Cook, pp. 159*n,* 161*n.*

28. Quoted in TPT, Pt. III, sec. 5, p. 9.

29. Quoted in TPT, Pt. III, sec. 5, pp. 8 - 9.

30. *The Monthly Review,* XLII, 86 (Sept. 1803), quoted in Tupper, *Royall Tyler,* p. 89.

31. "Retrospective Review" (Nov. 1810), pp. 344, 346.

32. TPT, Pt. III, sec. 5, p. 4. Also quoted in PEL, *Prose,* p. 46; see also p. 46, n. 1.

33. James Fenimore Cooper, review of *A New England Tale* by Maria Sedgewick, *Repository* (May 1822), rpt. in *Early Critical Essays (1820 - 1822),* ed. James F. Beard (Gainesville, Fla., 1955), pp. 336 - 37.

34. A. H. Quinn, *American Fiction* (New York, 1936), p. 24.
35. Carl Van Doren, *The American Novel/1789 - 1939* (New York, 1940), p. 8.
36. Alexander Cowie, *Rise of the American Novel* (New York, 1951), pp. 66 - 67.
37. Frank W. Chandler, *The Literature of Roguery* (New York, 1958), II, 405 - 406.
38. Mary Palmer Tyler, *Diary*, n. pag., [p. 114]; also see the entry for Nov. 14, 1824.
39. Hereafter, all references to and quotations from *The Bay Boy* refer to the edition in PEL, *Prose*, pp. 49 - 174. Quotations are used with the kind permission of Charles E. Tuttle Publishing Co., Inc.
40. See Edward Tyler to RT (Oct. 4, 1825), VHS; rpt. in PEL, *Prose*, p. 27.
41. Sidney Smith, review of Adam Seybert's *Statistical Annals. . .* , in *Edinburgh Review*, 33 (1820), 79. See PEL, *Prose*, p. 46, n. 1.
42. For discussions of the time period covered in *Captive*, see Chapman, p. 78; PEL, *Prose*, pp. 30 - 31, 37; and Tanselle, *Royall Tyler*, p. 206. In *Captive* (p. 43), Updike's birth date is given as July 16, 1762.
43. Possibly Dr. Sylvester Gardiner (1707 - 1786); see Chapman, p. 75, and PEL, *Prose*, p. 101.
44. The clock was installed in the 1770s; see PEL, *Prose*, p. 103*n*.
45. While an undergraduate at Harvard, Royall Tyler once fished with amusing results from a window. His hook snagged the wig of the college's president. See Sibley-Shipton, p. 318. The name Pompey is frequently used for servants and slaves, as in RT's *May Day in Town*.
46. Rpt. in PEL, *Verse*, pp. 160 - 64.
47. For a similar phrase, see *Captive*, p. 224; also see note 21, above.
48. Mary Palmer Tyler to Amelia Tyler (Jan. 19, 1825), unpubl. letter, VHS.
49. Hosea Beckley, quoted in Benjamin H. Hall, *History of Eastern Vermont, from its Earliest Settlement, to the Close of the Eighteenth Century* (New York, 1858), p. 714.

Chapter Five

1. The Tyler-Riley correspondence is reproduced in TPT, Pt. IV, pp. 80 - 82, 94 - 98, 101 - 102, 106 - 10, 124 - 25, 129 - 31. See A. L. Carson and H. L. Carson, "Outline for Thomas Pickman Tyler's *Memoir of Royall Tyler*," unpubl. MS, VHS.
2. Royall Tyler, *Reports of Cases Argued and Determined in the Supreme Court of Judicature of the State of Vermont with Cases of Practice and Rules of the Court* (New York: Isaac Riley, Vol. I in 1809; Vol. II in 1810; rpt. with annotations, St. Paul, Minn.: West Publishing, 1888). The law reports are discussed in our Ch. 6.

3. Royall Tyler, *THE YANKEY IN LONDON, BEING THE FIRST PART OF A SERIES OF LETTERS WRITTEN BY AN AMERICAN YOUTH, DURING NINE MONTHS' RESIDENCE IN THE CITY OF LONDON; ADDRESSED TO HIS FRIENDS IN AND NEAR BOSTON, MASSACHUSETTS* (New York: Isaac Riley, 1809). All quotations from *Yankey* refer to this edition.
4. See TPT, Pt. IV, p. 106; also see p. 108.
5. *Ibid.*, p. 107.
6. *Ibid.*, pp. 109 - 10.
7. *Ibid.*, p. 129.
8. See MPT, p. 295.
9. Rpt. in PEL, *Verse*, pp. 59 - 61, 83 - 84. The bluestockings were women with intellectual interests.
10. See Updike Underhill's disapproving attitude toward horse racing in *Captive*, Vol. I, Ch. 24.
11. Cf. Gulliver's disappointment with great figures of the past in Jonathan Swift, *Gulliver's Travels*, Bk. III, Ch. VIII. In the letters between Tyler and Senator Jonathan Robinson, there is an insistence on decorum in high places. See TPT, Pt. IV, p. 55 ("Maintain the national dignity. . ."). Also see TPT, Pt. III, sec. 8, pp. 16, 20; Pt. IV, pp. 120 *et passim*.
12. For other theories, see our Ch. 2, n. 36.
13. Tyler thought highly of the work of Macpherson, who inspired three of Tyler's poems: "The Scandinavian Hero," "Versification of a Passage from Ossian," and "Versification of a Dialogue from Ossian;" rpt. in PEL, *Verse*, pp. 127 - 30.
14. Anonymous Review, *Monthly Anthology and Boston Review*, VIII (Jan. 1810), p. 50. Tanselle attributes the review to William Tudor; see Tanselle's *Royall Tyler*, p. 271, n. 25. On the subject of letters from foreign travelers, see Martin Roth, *Comedy and America* (Port Washington, N.Y., 1976), p. 191, n. 2.
15. Anonymous Review, pp. 57 - 58.
16. TPT, Pt. IV, p. 112.
17. *Ibid.*, pp. 110 - 11.
18. Rourke, *Roots*, p. 123.
19. See Page Smith, *A New Age Now Begins*, Vol. I, Pt. I, Ch. 9, esp. pp. 143 - 44.
20. TPT, Pt. IV, pp. 143 - 50.
21. TPT, Pt. III, sec. 7, p. 18.
22. Similar statements about the contrast between a youthful America and an aging Europe can be found in J. Hector St. John de Crèvecoeur's *Letters from an American Farmer*, Letter III (1782), Washington Irving's *Sketch Book* (1819, 1820), and Henry David Thoreau's essay "Walking" (pub. 1862).
23. Rpt. in PEL, *Verse*, pp. 133 - 41.
24. Rpt. in PEL, *Prose*, pp. 214 - 16, 406 - 407.

25. Stein, pp. 471 - 72, n. 20.
26. For a discussion of similar views held by Thomas Jefferson, see Robert E. Spiller *et al.*, *Literary History of the United States* (New York, 1955), p. 151.
27. TPT, Pt. IV, p. 56.
28. Rourke, *Roots*, p. 124.
29. Tupper, "Royall Tyler," p. 90.

Chapter Six

1. MPT, p. 183.
2. *Ibid.*, p. 184.
3. For the reader's ease of reference, all quotations from and references to RT's prose, unless otherwise indicated, are taken from Marius B. Péladeau, ed., *The Prose of Royall Tyler* (Montpelier and Rutland, Vt.: Vermont Historical Society and The Charles E. Tuttle Company, 1972). Quotations are used with the kind permission of Charles E. Tuttle Publishing Co., Inc. The page numbers in parentheses in the text refer to this edition. In many cases we have also provided the original source of publication. Scholars may want to assess PEL's ed. by referring to G. Thomas Tanselle's review-essay, "The Editing of Royall Tyler," *Early American Literature*, IX, No. 1 (Spring 1974), 83 - 95.
4. This speech was published in the *Federal Galaxy*, IV, No. 82 (June 28, 1800), 4. It also was published separately as "AN ORATION, Pronounced At BENNINGTON, Vermont, *On the 22d February*, 1800. IN COMMEMORATION OF THE DEATH OF General GEORGE WASHINGTON/*By* ROYALL TYLER, *Esq*. (Walpole, N.H.: Printed for Thomas & Thomas by David Carlisle, 1800).
5. On this collaboration, see Ellis, p. 66.
6. Mott, *American Journalism*, p. 137. On Tyler and Dennie also see Frederick Hudson, *Journalism in the United States from 1690 to 1872* (1873; rpt. New York, 1968), pp. 228 - 29; and S. A. Bent, "Damon and Pythias." Many of the witty letters between Dennie and Tyler are cited at length in TPT; see especially Pt. III, sec. 5, pp. 4 - 9.
7. Quoted in Burbank and Moore, p. 647.
8. Ellis, p. 85. Also see PEL, *Prose*, pp. 281 - 82, 291. Tanselle questions the attribution in "The Editing of Royall Tyler," pp. 90 - 91.
9. Compare to "A Sermon and Prayer for Christmas Day," PEL, *Prose*, pp. 177 - 90.
10. Two RT poems also discuss clubs and associations. See "Irregular Supplicatory Address" (PEL, *Verse*, pp. 55 - 59) and "The Sun and the Bats. A Fable" (PEL, *Verse*, pp. 67 - 71).
11. See Joseph T. Buckingham's *Specimens of Newspaper Literature* (Boston, 1850), II, 177, 203. Buckingham's "Pertinax Period" was a conscious imitation of Colon & Spondee. See *Specimens*, I, 90.

12. *Ibid.*, II, 203.

13. *The Spirit of the Farmers' Museum, and Lay Preacher's Gazette* (Walpole, N.H.: Printed by D. & T. Carlisle for Thomas & Thomas, 1801). Dennie's copy of *Spirit* is in the Boston Public Library. Another copy of *Spirit* at the University of Vermont Library duplicates Dennie's notations.

14. The *Farmer's Weekly Museum* was issued from Apr. 11, 1793, to Oct. 15, 1810. See Mott, *American Journalism*, p. 137. David Carlisle also published *The Algerine Captive* in 1797.

15. See Buckingham, *Specimens*, II, 179, and Andrew P. Peabody, "Farmer's Weekly Museum," *Proceedings of the American Antiquarian Society*, VI, N.S. 122 (1890), p. 109.

16. Ellis, pp. 93 - 94.

17. *Ibid.*; also see Mott, *American Journalism*, pp. 137 - 38.

18. See Rourke, *Roots*, p. 122.

19. Thomas Paine was not popular in the RT household. Mary Tyler once threw Paine's *Age of Reason* into the fire. See MPT, pp. 252 - 53. On Paine as a favorite target of writers such as Washington Irving, see Roth, *Comedy and America*, pp. 70 - 71, 192, n. 25. Some of Irving's attacks on Paine appeared in Dennie's *Port Folio*.

20. A similar image was used earlier by Francis Hopkinson in his poem "The New Roof" (1787).

21. *Spirit*, pp. 266 - 69.

22. RT once considered, apparently seriously, writing a universal geography and a comic grammar. See letter dated Feb. 10, 1800, from RT to Nancrede in TPT, Pt. III, sec. 6, pp. 2 - 5.

23. On the significance of the *Port Folio*, see John Tebbel, *The Compact History of the American Newspaper* (New York, 1969), p. 249, and Mott, *Magazines*, pp. 123, 223 - 46. RT's work for the *Port Folio* can be partially identified. John E. Hall and his brother Harrison Hall (who were respectively editor and publisher of the *Port Folio* from 1816 to 1827) marked the authors' names in their personal volumes. The list indicates that RT contributed to the *Port Folio* five poems, two essays (one a Colon & Spondee), and the three essays headed "An Author's Evenings." See Randall, "Authors of *Port Folio* . . . ," pp. 379 - 416. Also see Tanselle, *Royall Tyler*, pp. 257 - 59, n. 12.

24. See Engelhart, p. 81.

25. *Massachusetts Spy*, XXV, No. 1258 (May 24, 1797), 4. Also see PEL, *Prose*, p. 301.

26. *Farmer's Weekly Museum*, V, No. 221 (June 26, 1797), 4. Also in PEL, *Prose*, pp. 302 - 303.

27. See *As You Like It* (II, 1).

28. RT used the correct name in *The Bay Boy;* see PEL, *Prose*, p. 114.

29. On RT and Buckingham, see TPT, Pt. III, sec. 8, pp. 5 - 15. Also see Joseph T. Buckingham, *Personal Memoirs and Recollections of Editorial Life* (Boston, 1852), I, 56.

30. Quoted in TPT, Pt. III, sec. 8, p. 8.
31. Quoted in *Ibid.*, p. 12.
32. Rpt. in PEL, *Verse*, pp. 146 - 48; see our Ch. 7.
33. RT used this scene in his *Island of Barrataria;* see our Ch. 3.
34. Tyler mentions Buckingham's request in RT, Day Book, unpubl. MS, VHS. See entry for March 6, 1817, p. 57. For Buckingham's attributions of "Postumi" see *Specimens*, II, 199.
35. Concerning these attributions, see PEL, *Prose*, pp. 320; 321, n. 53; 350, n. 80. Tanselle questions some of the Small Talk attributions. See "The Editing of Royall Tyler," p. 91. RT's "Day Book" (Dec. 28, 1817, p. 42) says, "Mr. Ide here in Eveng—wrote some small talk. . . ." MS at VHS. Tyler's entry is ambiguous.
36. *The Touchstone; or a Humble Modest Inquiry into the Nature of Religious Intolerance. Whether it ever existed? Whether those who practice it are conscious of it? Whether it is found in these regions? And the way to detect it ourselves.* By a member of the Berean Society. [Motto] Brattleborough, Vt. Published by Simeon Ide, 1817. See PEL, *Prose*, p. 290, n. 25. The subtitle is reminiscent of Jonathan Swift's satire "A Modest Proposal" (1729).
37. Simeon Ide to Thomas Pickman Tyler, n.d., unpubl. letter, VHS no. 62, MSS.9.
38. *Ibid.*
39. Tanselle, *Royall Tyler*, p. 269, n. 4. Also see PEL, *Prose*, pp. 290 - 91, n. 26.
40. TPT, Pt. III, sec. 8, p. 2; also see pp. 1 - 4.
41. *Ibid.*, p. 2. TPT spells the quack's name "John Johnstone," p. 1. RT's address is rpt. in PEL, *Prose*, pp. 406 - 407.
42. RT's *The Trial of Cyrus B. Dean, For the Murder of Jonathan Ormsby and Asa Marsh* (Burlington, Vt.: Samuel Mills, 1808).
43. On the effect of the embargo, see *Records of the Governor and Council of the State of Vermont,* V, 397; Appendix H, 472, 473. Also see TPT, Pt. IV, p. 60. Also see Catton and Catton, pp. 424 - 26.
44. TPT, Pt, IV. p. 63.
45. *Ibid.*, pp. 68, 69.
46. *Ibid.*, p. 69.
47. The charge is not reprinted in RT's pamphlet about the trial. The speech to the grand jury is in TPT, Pt. IV, pp. 70 - 76.
48. Crockett, *Vermont,* III, 141.
49. TPT, Pt. IV, p. 80. RT's letter is dated Nov. 8, 1808. RT had served on the court since 1801, seven years rather than nine years. Also see TPT, Pt. III, sec. 7, pp. 3 - 4.
50. *Ibid.*, Pt. IV, pp. 95 - 96.
51. RT, *Reports,* I, 181. See our Ch. 2, n. 13, for RT's personal attitude toward dueling.
52. H. S. Wardner, "Judge Jacob and His Dinah," *Vermonter*, 19, No. 5 - 6 (May-June 1914), 82. The case is summarized in Tyler, *Reports,* II, 192 - 201.

53. Quoted in TPT, Pt. IV, p. 131.

54. Quoted in Thomas Pickman Tyler, "Royall Tyler," p. 59. Also see TPT, Pt. IV, pp. 131 - 32.

55. Quoted in Tanselle, *Royall Tyler*, p. 40; also see p. 239, n. 100.

56. Quoted in TPT, Pt, IV, pp. 129 - 30.

57. *Ibid.*, p. 130.

58. Mary Palmer Tyler, *The Maternal Physician* . . . , 1st ed. (New York: Isaac Riley, 1811), 2nd ed. (Philadelphia: Lewis Adams, 1818).

59. No earlier book on child care by an American author is mentioned in Richard Harrison Shryock, *Medicine and Society in America: 1660 - 1860* (New York, 1960), or in Clarence Meyer, *American Folk Medicine* (New York, 1973).

60. Quoted in TPT, Pt. IV, p. 141.

61. Edward Tyler to RT (Oct. 4, 1824), unpubl. letter, VHS.

62. Mary Palmer Tyler, Diary (Apr. 19, 1825), [p. 118], VHS.

63. Mary Palmer Tyler to Edward Tyler (May 15, 1825), unpubl. letter, Box 50, VHS.

64. PEL, *Prose*, p. 443, n. 9.

65. *E.g.*, see *Bay Boy* in PEL, *Prose*, pp. 57 - 60, and the poem "Choice of a Wife," in PEL, *Verse*, p. 49. This favorite topic of RT's is also discussed in our Ch. 7.

66. RT-Nancrede letters, TPT, Pt. III, sec. 6, p. 2. The RT-Nancrede letters (TPT, Pt. III, sec. 6, pp. 2 - 21) are reprinted in G. Thomas Tanselle, "Author and Publisher in 1800: Letters of Royall Tyler and Joseph Nancrede," *Harvard Library Bulletin*, XV (Apr. 1967), 129 - 39. On Nancrede, also see Madeleine B. Stern, "Joseph Nancrede, Franco-American Bookseller-Publisher, 1761 - 1841," *The Papers of the Bibliographical Society of America*, 70 (First Quarter 1976), 1 - 88.

67. MPT, p. 265. Also see TPT, Pt. III, sec. 6, pp. 20 - 21.

68. *Ibid.*, pp. 18 - 20. Also see Tyler's satirical essay on simplified geographies and grammar books "The laudable rage, . . . " *Farmer's Weekly Museum*, Feb. 18, 1799; rpt. PEL, *Prose*, pp. 240 - 43.

69. One of RT's letters to Nancrede (Mar. 1800) says that the "Third story of the Tubwoman has I believe been told in some English Periodical, but I have touched it up in my own manner without—I believe—borrowing from any one." TPT, Pt. III, sec. 6, p. 17. This tale apparently has survived in a MS in the VHS, "The Historiette of the Tub Woman," which contains the first version of "The Tale of Five Pumpkins" (see our Ch. 3, Sec. VI).

70. Rourke, *Roots*, p. 122.

71. Peabody, *Farmer's Weekly Museum*, p. 116.

Chapter Seven

1. TPT, Pt. III, sec. 5, p. 16.

2. *Ibid.*, p. 6. Lope de Vega (1562 - 1635), the Spanish dramatist, is credited with having written as many as 1,800 plays.

3. Helen Tyler Brown, Intro. to Wilbur ed. of *Contrast*, p. xxviii.

4. Rpt. in PEL, *Verse*, pp. 3 - 5. For the reader's ease of reference, all quotations from and references to RT's poetry are taken from Marius B. Péladeau, ed., *The Verse of Royall Tyler* (Charlottesville, Va.: The University Press of Virginia, 1968). Quotations are used with the gracious permission of Walter Muir Whitehill for the Colonial Society of Massachusetts. The page numbers in parentheses refer to the University Press of Virginia edition. In many cases we have also provided the original source of publication. Scholars may want to assess Péladeau's edition by referring to G. Thomas Tanselle's review in *American Literature*, XLI, No. 1 (Mar. 1969), 117 - 19.

5. Drama as a moral instrument is the theme of Jeremy Collier's "Short View of the Immorality and Profaneness of the English Stage" (1698).

6. See the comment in MPT, p. 182.

7. *The Origin of Evil. An Elegy*, n. pag., 1793.

8. A CHRISTMAS HYMN, *COMPOSED BY THE HON. ROYALL TYLER, CHIEF JUSTICE OF THE STATE OF VERMONT, AND SUNG AT CLAREMONT, N.H. 1793*. Broadside, n.d., in the Dartmouth College Library, Hanover, N.H. The reference to Tyler as Chief Justice indicates that this broadside was printed no earlier than Oct. 1807.

9. TPT, Pt. III, sec. 5, p. 10. The letter from Coleman is dated Sept. 24 in the 1797 section. "Windsor Eulogy" might refer to "Windsor Ode," although the latter poem apparently was written in 1799.

10. *Ibid.*

11. Strephon and Delia are traditional names in pastoral verse. Tyler also uses the name Strephon in "The Test of Conjugal Love" (see PEL, *Verse*, pp. 34 - 35).

12. Buckingham, *Specimens*, II, 205.

13. *Ibid.*, II, 106.

14. See the head note in PEL, *Verse*, p. 84. Tyler used a similar idea in "Epigram," a Colon & Spondee poem *(Eagle*, Nov. 17, 1794); rpt. in PEL, *Verse*, p. 33.

15. TPT, Pt. III, sec. 8, p. 12.

16. RT to Dennie (Oct. 7, 1795), MS in New Hampshire Historical Society.

17. TPT, Pt. III, sec. 8, p. 10.

18. PEL, *Verse*, p. 143. RT's introductory essay to the poem is rpt. in PEL, *Prose*, p. 416.

19. Cf. Hamlet's speech to the players, Act III, Sc. II, 11. 1 - 50.

20. TPT, Pt. III, sec. 8, p. 11.

21. PEL, *Prose*, p. 141. In meter, imagery, and diction, "Come, Thalia" is reminiscent of John Milton's "L'Allegro" *(c.* 1631).

22. See *Theatre Arts* (July 1, 1945), p. 417; and *Colliers*, 128, No. 20 (July 7, 1951), p. 20.

23. See TPT, Pt. III, sec. 7, p. 25.

24. *Ibid.*, pp. 36 - 7. Also see Howard H. Martin, "The Fourth of July Oration," *Quarterly Journal of Speech*, XLIV (Dec. 1958), 393 - 401.

25. *Captive*, p. 124. Also see the poem on freedom in *Captive*, Vol. II, Ch. 16, p. 168.
26. See William Coleman's reference to "Windsor Eulogy," above, n. 9.
27. Buckingham, *Specimens*, II, 207.
28. For American attitudes toward France in the 1790s, see Morison and Commager, I, 371 - 81.
29. Also rpt. in Buckingham, *Specimens*, II, 207 - 209.
30. Undated broadside, Wilbur collection, UVM.
31. Parts of "The Mantle of Washington" appeared in W. J. Coates, *Favorite Vermont Poems*, Series One (No. Montpelier, Vt.: Driftwind Press, 1928), p. 6; also see *The Driftwind*, IV (Sept. 1929), 6.
32. Also see PEL, *Prose*, p. 164.
33. Also see *Captive*, p. 105.
34. *Ibid.*, p. 177.
35. PEL, *Prose*, p. 298. A simliar treatment of animals of darkness as political symbols can be found in Washington Irving. See discussion in Martin Roth, *Washington Irving's Contributions to* The Corrector (Minneapolis, 1968), p. 33.
36. See *Captive*, pp. 48, 50; and *Bay Boy*, in PEL, *Prose*, pp. 84, 88. Also see RT's Saunterer essay (Sept. 5, 1794), which attacks associations that "publish their learned lumber" but "are not commonly the authors of any great improvements" (PEL, *Prose*, p. 299). Also compare Jonathan Swift, *Gulliver's Travels*, Bk. III, and Samuel Johnson, *Rambler*, No. 82 (Dec. 29, 1750).
37. M. Ray Adams, "Della Cruscanism in America," *PMLA*, LXXIX (June 1964), 259. Also see M. Ray Adams, "Robert Merry, Political Romanticist," *Studies in Romanticism*, II (Autumn 1962), 27 - 37. Tyler's comments on Della Cruscanism can also be found in his prose; see *Yankey*, Letter III and our Ch. 6, Sec. II.
38. James L. Onderdonk, *History of American Verse (1610 - 1897)* (Chicago, 1901), p. 114; also see p. 117.
39. Fred Lewis Pattee, *The First Century of American Literature / 1770 - 1870* (New York, 1966), p. 107.
40. Onderdonk, p. 113.
41. Quoted in Pattee, *First Century*, p. 112.
42. Adams, "Della Cruscanism," p. 261.
43. An Englishwoman named Hannah Cowley (1743 - 1809) published her Della Cruscan poetry under the pseudonym of "Anna Matilda."
44. Adams, "Della Cruscanism," p. 261.
45. See Letter III, pp. 12 - 13.
46. Adams, "Della Cruscanism," p. 261.
47. Macpherson is discussed in *Yankey*, Letter XXXIII, pp. 127 - 30.
48. Tanselle corrects "flies" in PEL to the more effective "flees," as we have done here. See Tanselle's review of *The Verse of Royall Tyler*, p. 118.
49. Rpt. in PEL, *Verse*, pp. 114 - 15. Attributed to Tyler in the Hall files; see Randall, p. 411.

50. See our Ch. 6, Sec. III, on the "Old Simon" columns.

51. The sonnet is rpt. in PEL, *Verse*, pp. 14 - 15; "Old Simon" is on pp. 123 - 24; and "Hymn" is on pp. 119 - 21.

52. Rpt. in PEL, *Verse*, pp. 131 - 32.

53. Cf. the praise of the village preacher in Oliver Goldsmith's "Deserted Village" (1770).

54. Cf. Wordsworth's "I Wandered Lonely as a Cloud" (1807).

55. Other comments by Tyler on the legal profession can be found in *The Island of Barrataria, The Judgement of Solomon,* and "The Chestnut Tree."

56. *Valedictory Address, Delivered . . . at the Quarterly Examination of Miss Peck's Select School, by Thomas Pickman Tyler,—(Aged Eight Years).* Broadside, [*c.* 1824]. Rpt. in Henry Burnham, *Brattleboro, Windham County, Vermont,* ed. Abby Maria Hemenway (Brattleboro, Vt.: D. Leonard, 1880), pp. 84 - 85. Also in PEL, *Verse,* pp. 189 - 93. There is some question about the date of *Valedictory Address* (see Tanselle, *Royall Tyler,* p. 214). In the diary of Mary Palmer Tyler (entry for Saturday, Oct. 23, 1824), she reports, "Last Thursday Miss Peck had a quarterly examination of her Pupils. . . . Pickman spoke a valedictory address—written for the occasion by his Father—" [p. 111], VHS.

57. Burnham, p. 85, attempts to identify the girls.

58. For example, see Alexander Pope's "Ode on Solitude" (1717). *Otium* is a literary attitude that goes back to Horace and appears in Elizabethan, seventeenth-century, and eighteenth-century English poetry.

59. Tanselle does not refer to the poem in *Royall Tyler* or in the review of PEL's *Verse*. PEL attributes the poem to RT; see *Verse*, p. 236.

60. See PEL, *Prose*, p. 42.

61. Unpubl. letter, VHS.

62. RT, *The Chestnut Tree, Or a Sketch of Brattleborough (East Village) At the Close of the Twentieth Century, Being an Address to a Horse Chestnut Presented to the Author by the Rev. A. L. Baury. . . .* (No. Montpelier, Vt.: Driftwind Press, 1931). Rev. Baury was a family friend of the Tylers.

63. For a discussion of the various texts of "The Chestnut Tree," see PEL, *Verse,* p. 194, and Tanselle, *Royall Tyler,* pp. 263 - 64, n. 51.

64. RT, whose face was disfigured by cancer in his last years, used a similar image in "A Valedictory Address" (PEL, *Verse*, p. 190, 1.39).

65. On industrial conditions in the United States during the early nineteenth century, see Morison and Commager, I, 426 - 27, 502 - 505.

66. Unemployment, rural poverty, and female paupers are also depicted in Oliver Goldsmith's "The Deserted Village" (1770) and George Crabbe's "The Village" (1783) and "The Borough" (1810).

67. The stale bachelor was a stock figure in periodical literature of the times, usually treated in a harsh, critical, or satirical manner. See Roth, *Comedy and America*, pp. 38 - 39. RT, however, makes his portrait a study in pathos.

68. Compare RT's "wight" with Chaucer's Clerk of Oxenford ("Prologue" to *The Canterbury Tales)* or Samuel Johnson's scholar in *Rambler,* No. 83 (Jan. 1, 1751).

69. See Edward Young's "The Complaint, or Night Thoughts" (1742 - 45), Robert Blair's "The Grave" (1743), and Thomas Gray's "Elegy Written in a Country Churchyard" (1751) for examples of the Graveyard School of poetry.

70. The most famous early comments on industrialism in England are Thomas Hood's "Song of the Shirt" (1843), Elizabeth Barrett Browning's "Cry of the Children" (1844), and Charles Dickens's *Hard Times* (1854). In America, early statements appear in Herman Melville's essay "The Paradise of Bachelors and the Tartarus of Maids" (1855) and Rebecca Harding Davis's story "Life in the Iron Mills" (1861).

71. Buckingham, *Specimens,* II, 203.

72. TPT, Pt. II, sec. 4, p. 3.

73. Bent, p. 672.

74. Tupper, "Royall Tyler," p. 92.

75. For a discussion of "The Wolf and Wooden Beauty," see our Ch. 4, Sec. VI.

Chapter Eight

1. TPT, Pt. III, sec. 8, p. 8.
2. Quoted in Randall, p. 380.
3. TPT, Pt. III, sec. 5, pp. 6, 9.
4. Rourke, *Roots,* p. 124.
5. Cooper, quoted in Beard, pp. 336 - 37.
6. Pattee, *The First Century of American Literature,* p. 221.

Selected Bibliography

This selected bibliography includes references to all of the materials by Royall Tyler which appeared separately as books, pamphlets, or broadsides. The major sources on RT are also listed. The reader is referred to the footnotes for works which deal tangentially with RT and his times.

PRIMARY SOURCES

(Arranged Chronologically by Date of Publication)

SONGS in the Comic Opera of Two Acts, called, MAY DAY IN TOWN. Written by the Author of The Contrast. New York: H. Gaine, 1787. Rpt. in K. S. Jarvis, "Royall Tyler's Lyrics for *May Day in Town*" *(q.v.).*

THE CONTRAST, A Comedy; in Five Acts: written by a citizen of the United States. . . . Philadelphia: Prichard & Hall, 1790. G.T. Tanselle in "Some Uncollected Authors XLII" *(q.v.)* gives the locations of twelve first editions of *The Contrast.* There is also an edition at the Clements Library at the University of Michigan.

Some editions of *The Contrast:*

McKEE, THOMAS J., ed. Intro. by Thomas J. McKee. New York: The Dunlap Society, 1887.

McKEE ed. reissued in facsim. New York: Burt Franklin, 1970.

WILBUR, JAMES BENJAMIN, ed. With *History of George Washington's Copy* by James Benjamin Wilbur and Intro. by Helen Tyler Brown. Boston: Houghton Mifflin, 1920. George Washington's personal, autographed copy is at the UVM Library.

WILBUR ed. reissued. New York: AMS Press, 1970.

The play appears in numerous anthologies, including:

QUINN, ARTHUR HOBSON. *Representative American Plays.* New York: Appleton, 1917.

HALLINE, ALLAN G. *American Plays.* New York: American Book Company, 1935.

BURBANK, REX J., and MOORE, JACK B. *The Literature of Early America.* Columbus, O.: Charles E. Merrill Books, 1967.

BRADLEY, SCULLEY, *et al., The American Tradition in Literature.* 4th ed. New York: Grossett & Dunlap, distr. by W. W. Norton, 1974.

The Origin of Evil. An Elegy. n. pag., 1793. Copy at American Antiquarian Society, Worcester, Mass.

A Christmas Hymn, Composed by the Hon. Royall Tyler, Chief Justice of the State of Vermont, *and Sung at Claremont,* N. H. *1793.* Broadside.

Copy at Dartmouth College Library. This work was printed no earlier than October 1807; see Ch. 7, n. 8.

The Algerine Captive; or, the Life and Adventures of Doctor Updike Underhill: Six years a prisoner among the Algerines. 2 vols. Walpole, N.H.: David Carlisle, 1797. Available in University Microfilms, American Culture Series No. 241 (Roll 25).

Other editions of *The Algerine Captive:*

Selections rpt. in *Farmer's Weekly Museum* (Aug. 14 and 21, 1797).

2 vols. London: G. and J. Robinson, 1802.

Serialized in *The Lady's Magazine* (London), XXXV (1804).

1 vol. Hartford, Conn.: Peter B. Gleason, 1816.

1 vol. facsim. of 1797 ed. Intro. by Jack B. Moore. Gainesville, Fla.: Scholars' Facsimiles & Reprints, 1967.

COOK, DON L., ed. New Haven, Conn.: College & University Press, 1970.

Convivial Song, Sung at Windsor, on the Evening of the Fourth of July. / Composed for the occasion—by R. Tyler. Broadside, 1799. Copy at UVM Library.

AN ORATION Pronounced At BENNINGTON, *Vermont*, On the 22d February, 1800. *IN COMMEMORATION OF THE DEATH OF General GEORGE WASHINGTON* / By ROYALL TYLER, Esq. Walpole, N.H.: Printed for Thomas & Thomas by David Carlisle, 1800. Copies at VHS, UVM Library, etc.

The Trial of Cyrus B. Dean, For the Murder of Jonathan Ormsby and Asa Marsh, Before the Supreme Court of Judicature of the State of Vermont. . . . Burlington, Vt.: Samuel Mills, 1808. Copy at UVM Library.

The YANKEY IN LONDON, being the first part of A SERIES OF LETTERS Written by an American Youth, During Nine Months' Residence in the City of London; Addressed to His Friends in and Near Boston, Massachusetts. New York: Isaac Riley, 1809. Copy at UVM Library.

Reports of Cases Argued and Determined in the Supreme Court of Judicature of the State of Vermont with Cases of Practice and Rules of the Court. Commencing with the Nineteenth Century. 2 vols. New York: Isaac Riley, 1809 - 1810. Rpt. with annotations. St. Paul, Minn.: West Publishing Co., 1888.

The Touchstone, or a Humble Modest Inquiry into the Nature of Religious Intolerance. . . . So. Brattleborough, Vt.: Simeon Ide, 1817. No longer extant.

A Valedictory Address, Delivered . . . at the Quarterly Examination of Miss Peck's Select School. By Thomas Pickman Tyler,—(Aged Eight Years). Broadside, [*c*. 1824]. See Ch. 7, n. 56, about the date of publication.

The Chestnut Tree, Or a Sketch of Brattleborough (East Village) At the Close of the Twentieth Century, Being an Address to a Horse Chest-

nut, Presented to the Author by the Rev. A. L. Baury, Episcopal Clergyman in Guilford, Vermont. Intro. by Walter John Coates. No. Montpelier, Vt.: Driftwind Press, 1931.

Four Plays by Royall Tyler [The Island of Barrataria, The Origin of the Feast of Purim, Joseph and His Brethren, and *The Judgement of Solomon].* Ed. Arthur Wallace Peach and George Floyd Newbrough. Vol. 15 of *America's Lost Plays,* ed. Barrett H. Clark. Princeton: Princeton Univ. Press, 1941. Rpt., bound with Vol. 16 of *America's Lost Plays.* Bloomington, Ind.: Indiana Univ. Press, 1965.

The Verse of Royall Tyler. Ed. Marius B. Péladeau. Charlottesville, Va.: The University Press of Virginia, 1968. (Reviewed by G. T. Tanselle—*q.v.)* Rpt. from *Publications of the Colonial Society of Massachusetts Transactions,* Vol. 44 (1967).

The Prose of Royall Tyler. Ed. Marius B. Péladeau. Montpelier and Rutland, Vt.: Vermont Historical Society and Charles E. Tuttle Co., 1972. (Reviewed by G. T. Tanselle—*q.v.)* RT's poetry and prose appeared in many periodicals. The footnotes list a number of these publications. Other lists may be found in Péladeau's two editions and in the critical biography by Tanselle. Many of RT's prose and poetic works were reprinted in *The Spirit of the Farmers' Museum,* Walpole, N.H.: Printed for Thomas & Thomas by D. & T. Carlisle, 1801; See our Ch. 6, n. 13.

Unpublished material relating to RT can be found at the VHS. Of greatest value to biographers is the MS "Memoir of Royall Tyler," by his son Thomas Pickman Tyler *(q.v.).* Also valuable are Mary Palmer Tyler's autobiography (published in 1925 as *Grandmother Tyler's Book—q.v.)* and the manuscript of her diary (see G. F. Newbrough, "Mary Tyler's Journal"), RT's Day Book, several MSS in RT's or Mary Palmer Tyler's handwriting, Tyler family letters, copies of *Barrataria,* the religious dramas, *Bay Boy,* etc. (Listed in Anon., "The Royall Tyler Collection"—*q.v.;* also see listing in Tanselle, *Royall Tyler,* pp. 215 - 17.)

SECONDARY SOURCES

1. Periodical Material

ADAMS, M. RAY. "Della Cruscanism in America." *PMLA,* LXXIX (June 1964), 259 - 65. A good discussion of this poetic phenomenon and its influence.

ANON. "The American on the Stage." *Scribner's Monthly,* XVIII, No. 3 (July 1879), 321 - 33. Discusses Yankee types, including RT's Jonathan.

ANON. "Article 3. *The Yankey in London. . . .*" *Monthly Anthology and Boston Review,* VIII (Jan. 1810), 50 - 58. Calls *Yankey* "useless"; the humorless reviewer comments that any well read person could have written the book without going abroad.

ANON. "Novels and Romances." *Monthly Magazine,* Supp. 13 (July 20, 1802), p. 659. One-paragraph reference to *The Algerine Captive* as "very entertaining . . . some shrewd remarks on the events of the present day."

ANON. "Our First Truly National Play: *The Contrast*." *Delineator*, 85 (July 1914), 7. Brief, unreliable.

ANON. "Retrospective Review. Article 27. / *The Algerine Captive*. . . ." *Monthly Anthology and Boston Review*, XI (Nov. 1810), 344 - 47. Criticizes RT for his "perpetual invective against classical learning" and his "cowardly mode of attacking revelation."

ANON. Reviews of *The Contrast* (selected):

"Candour." *Daily Advertiser* (Apr. 18, 1787). Rpt. in *The American Theatre, 1752 - 1934*, Montrose J. Moses and John Mason Brown, eds. (New York: Norton, 1934), pp. 24 - 25. The first review in an American publication of a play by an American; a well-written and perceptive comment, which takes RT to task for several faults of dramaturgy.

"Philo Dramaticus." New York *Independent Journal* (May 5, 1787).

Worcester (Mass.) *Magazine*, III (May 1787), 61.

The Maryland Gazette or, the Baltimore Advertiser (Nov. 13, 1787), p. 3.

"Theatrical Intelligence." *The Maryland Journal and Baltimore Advertiser* (Nov. 16, 1787), p. 3.

"Impartial Review." *Universal Asylum and Columbian Magazine* (Phila.), V (1790), 117 - 20.

Also see modern reviews by H. Clurman, C. Barnes, and W. Kerr *(q.v.)*.

ANON. "The Royall Tyler Collection." *Proceedings of the Vermont Historical Society*, N.S. IV:1 (1936), 3 - 4. Brief description of RT collection at VHS.

BALCH, MARSTON. "Jonathan the First." *Modern Language Notes*, XLVI, No. 5 (May 1931), 281 - 88. A valuable discussion of Jonathen in Joseph Atkinson's *A Match for a Widow*. Jonathen is similar to RT's Jonathan, but Balch concludes, ". . . the facts, if known, would credit full originality to the American playwright," *i.e.*, to RT.

BARNES, CLIVE. "Stage: 1787's 'The Contrast' Returns with Spirit." *New York Times* (Nov. 28, 1972), p. 51. Prefers RT's play to the musical adaptation.

BENRIMO, A. "The First American Dramatist." *Dramatic Magazine*, I (May 1880), 57 - 59. Brief article, popular approach.

BENT, S. ARTHUR. "Damon and Pythias Among Our Early Journalists." *New England Magazine*, N.S. 19 (Aug. 1896), 666 - 75. Discusses RT and Dennie, their friendship, collaboration, and separate careers. Not reliable on RT.

BISHOP, W. "First American Comedy; 'The Contrast.'" *The Mentor*, XV:39 (Jan. 1928), 30. Brief, for nonspecialists only.

BROWN, HERBERT R. "Sensibility in Eighteenth-Century American Drama." *American Literature*, IV (Mar. 1932), 47 - 60. Maria and Manly as sentimental figures; a valuable imterpretation.

BROWN, ROGER H. "A Vermont Republican Urges War: Royall Tyler, 1812, and the Safety of Republican Government." *Vermont History*, 36, No.

1 (Winter 1968), 13 - 18. Discusses and reproduces RT's letter to Congressman James Fisk.

CARSON, HERBERT L., and ADA LOU CARSON. "The Jews, Royall Tyler, and America's Divided Mind." *American Jewish Archives,* XXVIII, No. 1 (Apr. 1976), 79 - 84. Discusses RT's portrayal of Jews in *Captive.*

CLURMAN, HAROLD. "Theatre." *Nation* (Dec 18, 1972), p. 637. Like Barnes, Clurman preferred RT's play to the modern adaptation.

COATES, WALTER J. "Poets and Poetry of Vermont." *Vermonter,* 34, No. 3 (Mar. 1929), 35 - 41. Devotes only a column to "the greatest and most original figure in early Vermont literature . . . Royall Tyler."

DELL, ROBERT M., and CHARLES A. HUGUENIN. "Vermont's Royall Tyler in New York's John Street Theatre: A Theatrical Hoax Exploded." *Vermont History,* XXXVIII (Spring 1970), 103 - 12. "Correcting an error about the internal appearance of the theatre. . . ."

DENNIS, LARRY R. "Legitimizing the Novel: Royall Tyler's *The Algerine Captive.*" *Early American Literature,* IX, No. 1 (Spring 1974), 71 - 80. A general discussion.

FORSYTHE, ROBERT S. " 'The Algerine Captive,' 1802." *Notes and Queries,* CLXXII (May 29, 1937), 389 - 90. Answers question by W. Roberts, CLXXII (Apr. 17, 1937), p. 282. Also see comment by Albert Matthews, CLXXII (May 22, 1937), p. 374.

GUSOW, MEL. "Early Americana in Hamptons." *New York Times* (July 16, 1976), sec. C, p. 4. About a bicentennial production of *The Contrast* in the Stimac musical adaptation.

HORNIBROOK, J. L. "America's First Comedy." *Landmark,* XIV (1932), 391 - 92. Too brief for value.

JARVIS, KATHERINE SCHALL. "Royall Tyler's Lyrics for *May Day in Town.*" *Harvard Library Bulletin,* XXIII, No. 2 (Apr. 1975), 186 - 98. A valuable discussion of Ms. Jarvis's discovery. Reprints the lyrics.

KERR, WALTER. "Why Do They Speak?" *New York Times* (Dec. 24, 1972), sec. II. p. 7. "Well sung and directorially camped"; concludes of RT's play, "Someone else will do it sometime and maybe next time do it right."

KILLHEFFER, MARIE. "A Comparison of the Dialect of 'The Biglow Papers' with the Dialect of Four Yankee Plays." *American Speech* (Feb. 1928), pp. 222 - 36. Statistical analysis concludes that RT "shows the slightest attempt to indicate dialect but by far the largest proportion of dialect words. . . ."

KOLLER, JOHN D. "American Revolution Theatre Scene / Getting the Contrast into Focus or Early American Theatre Shafted Royally." *The Massachusetts Spy* (Apr. 1974), p. 7. Cheerful debunking.

LAUBER, JOHN. "*The Contrast:* A Study in the Concept of Innocence." *English Language Notes,* I (Sept. 1963), 33 - 37. Good, brief discussion of RT's play and R. W. B. Lewis's theories about the American Adam.

MAYO, LIDA. "Miss Adams in Love." *American Heritage,* XVI (Feb. 1965),

36 - 39, 80 - 89. Interesting account of Nabby's romances with RT and with Col. William Smith.

NETHERCOT, ARTHUR H. "The Dramatic Background of Royall Tyler's *The Contrast.*" *American Literature*, XII (Jan. 1941), 435 - 46. Tries to reconstruct RT's knowledge of drama prior to composing *The Contrast.*

NEWBROUGH, GEORGE FLOYD. "Mary Tyler's Journal." *Vermont Quarterly*, 20 (Jan. 1952), 19 - 31. Brief discussion and some reprints from a valuable research aid.

PÉLADEAU, MARIUS B. "Royall Tyler and Ethan Allen's Appendix to *Reason the Only Oracle of Man.*" *Vermont History*, XXXVI, No. 3 (Summer 1968), 155 - 58. Discusses and reproduces a brief letter from Ethan Allen to RT, apparently describing a plan to issue Allen's work by subscription.

______. "Royall Tyler and the University of Vermont." *Vermont History*, XLII, No. 1 (Winter 1974), 22 - 33. Useful discussion of RT's contributions to UVM.

______. "Royall Tyler's *Other* Plays." *New England Quarterly*, 40 (Mar. 1967), 48 - 60. Valuable survey. Compare these attributions by Péladeau to the ones by Tanselle, especially in "Royall Tyler, Judith Sargent Murray. . ." *(q.v.)*.

RANDALL, RANDOLPH C. "Authors of *Port Folio* Revealed by the Hall Files." *American Literature*, XI (Jan. 1940), 379 - 416. Helpful; indicates RT's contributions to Dennie's magazine.

SIEBERT, DONALD T., JR. "Royall Tyler's 'Bold Example': *The Contrast* and the English Comedy of Manners," *Early American Literature*, XIII:1 (Spring 1978), pp. 3 - 11. Views Tyler's play as a " 'bold attempt' to create a truly original comedy within the formal context of seventeenth and eighteenth-century English drama. . . . [Tyler] still deserves more critical applause for what he succeeded in doing than he has received." (p. 5).

STEIN, ROGER B. "Royall Tyler and the Question of Our Speech." *New England Quarterly*, 38 (Dec. 1965), 454 - 74. Good discussion of the "linguistic orientation of *The Contrast*. . . ."

TAFT, RUSSELL. "Royall Tyler." *Green Bag*, XX (Jan. 1908), 1 - 5. Stresses RT's career as an attorney.

TANSELLE, G. THOMAS. "Attribution of Authorship in 'The Spirit of the Farmers' Museum' (1801)." *Papers of the Bibliographical Society of America*, LIX (Apr. 1965), 170 - 76. Discusses the Boston Public Library's copy of *Spirit*, marked by Dennie. Like all of Tanselle's work, this article is scholarly, precise, and helpful.

______. "Author and Publisher in 1800: Letters of Royall Tyler and Joseph Nancrede." *Harvard Library Bulletin*, XV (Apr. 1967), 129 - 39. Discusses and reprints the correspondence (based on TPT).

______. "Early American Fiction in England: The Case of *The Algerine*

Captive." *Papers of the Bibliographical Society of America*, LIX (Oct. 1965), 367 - 84. Credits Charles Brockden Brown's *Ormond* as first American novel to be reprinted in England; places *Captive* as second. *Captive* (1797) was published earlier than *Ormond* (1799) in America. *Ormond* was published in 1800 in England; *Captive*, in 1802.

———. "The Editing of Royall Tyler." *Early American Literature*, IX, No. 1 (Spring 1974), 83 - 95. A valuable "Review Essay" about M. B. Péladeau's edition of RT's prose *(q.v.)*.

———. "Royal Tyler, Judith Sargent Murray, and *The Medium*." *New England Quarterly*, XLI (Mar. 1968), 115 - 17. Attributes *The Medium* to Mrs. Murray; cf. Péladeau's "Royall Tyler's *Other* Plays" *(q.v.)*.

———. "Some Uncollected Authors XLII / Royall Tyler, 1757 - 1826." *Book Collector*, XV (Autumn 1966), 303 - 20. RT has since been collected by Péladeau *(q.v.)*; but the bibliographical information in this article is useful.

———. Review of *The Verse of Royall Tyler*, ed. Marius B. Péladeau. *American Literature*, XLI, No. 1 (Mar. 1969), 117 - 19. Valuable commentary.

TUPPER, FREDERICK. "The Poetry of Royall Tyler." *Driftwind*, II (June 1927), 10 - 11. A brief tribute.

———. "Royall Tyler," *Proceedings of the Vermont Historical Society*, IV (1928), 65 - 101. Good, occasionally inaccurate survey.

TYLER, THOMAS PICKMAN. "Royall Tyler." *Proceedings of The Vermont Bar Association*, I (1878 - 1881), 44 - 62; also in *Argus and Patriot* (Montpelier, Vt.), N.S. XXIX (Nov. 5, 1879). A survey based upon TPT's projected biography.

WARDNER, H. S. "The Wilbur Edition of 'The Contrast,' " *Vermonter*, XXVI (Feb. 1921), 40 - 41. An enthusiastic review.

WHITE, PLINY H. "Royall Tyler," in "Early Poets of Vermont." *Proceedings of the Vermont Historical Society, 1917 - 1918* (1920), pp. 108 - 19. Useful survey of RT's verse.

2. Books

BUCKINGHAM, JOSEPH T. *Specimens of Newspaper Literature: with Personal Memoirs, Anecdotes, and Reminiscences*. 2 vols. Boston: C. C. Little and J. Brown, 1850. Reprints several works by RT.

BURNHAM, HENRY. *Brattleboro, Windham County, Vermont*. Ed. Abby Maria Hemenway. Brattleboro, Vt.: D. Leonard, 1880. Good account of RT.

BUTTERFIELD, LYMAN H., WENDELL D. GARRETT, and MARC FRIEDLAENDER. *The Earliest Diary of John Adams*. Cambridge, Mass.: Harvard Univ. Press, 1966. See "Intro." for a fascinating account of the discovery of Adams's diary among RT's papers.

CABOT, MARY R. *Annals of Brattleboro, 1681 - 1895*. Brattleboro, Vt.: E. L. Hildreth, vol. I—1921; vol. II—1922. Valuable materials on the Tylers and their neighbors. See esp. Vol. I, Ch. XXIII.

CHAPMAN, BERTRAND WILLIAM. "The Nativism of Royall Tyler." M.A. thesis, Univ. of Vermont, 1933. Good work on sources; some valuable analyses.

CHITTENDEN, L. E. *Personal Reminiscences, 1840 - 90.* New York: Richmond, Croscup & Co., 1893. The discovery of the Washington copy of *The Contrast.*

COATES, WALTER J. *Favorite Vermont Poems,* Series One. North Montpelier, Vt.: Driftwind Press, 1928. Reprints some of RT's verse.

______, and FREDERICK TUPPER. *Vermont Verse: An Anthology.* Brattleboro, Vt.: Stephen Daye Press, 1931. Reprints several of RT's poems.

COOPER, JAMES FENIMORE. *Early Critical Essays.* Ed. James F. Beard. Gainesville, Fla.: Scholars' Facsimiles and Reprints, 1955. Includes interesting praise of RT's *Captive.*

COWIE, ALEXANDER. *The Rise of the American Novel.* New York: American Book Co., 1951. Complimentary discussion of RT's style in *The Algerine Captive.*

CROCKETT, WALTER H. *Vermonters, A Book of Biographies.* Brattleboro: Stephen Daye Press, 1932. Contains a brief article on "Royall Tyler" by Frederick Tupper.

DEMING, LEONARD. *Catalogue of the Principal Officers of Vermont, as Connected with its Political History, from 1778 - 1851.* Middlebury, Vt.: Published by the Author, 1851. Useful references to RT and his colleagues.

DENNIE, JOSEPH. *The Letters of Joseph Dennie.* Ed. Laura Green Pedder. Orono, Maine: Univ. of Maine, 1936. Valuable work, including some material taken from TPT's manuscript.

DODGE, PRENTISS C. *Encyclopedia of Vermont Biography.* Burlington, Vt.: Ullery Publishing Co., 1912. Brief references to the Tylers.

DUYCKINCK, EVERT A., and GEORGE L. DUYCKINCK, eds. *Cyclopedia of American Literature.* New York: Scribners, 1860. A standard reference work. Several dates are incorrect in the article on RT, including the date of the presentation of *The Contrast.*

ELLIS, H. MILTON. *Joseph Dennie and His Circle.* Austin, Tex.: Univ. of Texas, 1915. Good information on RT's friend and collaborator.

ENGELHART, CARL WILLIAM. "An Historical and Critical Study of Royall Tyler." M.A. thesis, Univ. of Minnesota, 1943. A valuable discussion.

GILMAN, M. D. *Bibliography of Vermont.* Burlington, Vt.: The Free Press Association, 1897. Brief biographies of both Mary and RT.

GRAHAM, J[OHN] A[NDREW]. *A Descriptive Sketch of the Present State of Vermont. . . .* London: Printed for the author by Henry Fry, 1797. Accolades for Attorney Tyler.

HALLINE, ALLAN GATES. *Main Currents of Thought in American Drama.* Ph.D. Diss., Univ. of Wisconsin, 1936. Very good analysis of RT's nationalism.

HEMENWAY, ABBY MARIA. *Poets and Poetry of Vermont.* Boston: Brown, Taggard, and Chase, 1860. Contains several of RT's poems.

JONES, CLAUD E. *Prefaces to Three 18th Century Novels.* Los Angeles: Univ. of Calif. Press, 1957. Contains RT's preface to *The Algerine Captive.*

LEARY, LEWIS. *Soundings.* Athens, Ga.: Univ. of Georgia Press, 1975. Section on RT, general information and opinion, pp. 83 - 95.

ODELL, GEORGE C. D. *Annals of the New York Stage,* Vol. I. New York: Columbia Univ. Press, 1927. Useful records. See esp. pp. 255 - 59, 274.

QUINN, ARTHUR HOBSON. *American Fiction.* New York: Appleton-Century-Crofts, 1936. Good discussion of RT by an eminent scholar.

———. *A History of American Drama from the Beginning to the Civil War.* New York: F. S. Crofts & Co., 1946. A major survey; valuable comments on *The Contrast.*

———. "Royall Tyler" in *Dictionary of American Biography,* XIX (1936), 95 - 97. An excellent brief survey.

QUINN, JAMES JOSEPH, JR. "The Jonathan Character in the American Drama," Ph.D., diss., Columbia, 1955. Good survey of RT's Yankee and his subsequent influence.

REED, PERLEY ISAAC. *The Realistic Presentation of American Characters in Native Plays Prior to Eighteen Seventy.* Columbus, O.: *Ohio State Univ. Bulletin,* No. 26 (May 1918). Especially valuable references to *The Contrast.*

ROURKE, CONSTANCE. *The Roots of American Culture and Other Essays.* Ed. Van Wyck Brooks. Port Washington, N.Y.: Kennikat Press, Inc., 1965. Worthwhile comments on RT's *Yankey,* but Rourke's description of the work is not completely accurate.

SEILHAMER, GEORGE O. *History of American Theatre.* 3 vols. Philadelphia: Globe Printing House, 1888 - 91. Some valuable primary information about the productions of RT's plays.

SILVERMAN, KENNETH. *A Cultural History of the American Revolution.* New York: Thomas Y. Crowell Co., 1976. Discusses *The Contrast* as one sign that America was developing its own cultural life.

SLOUT, WILLIAM LAWRENCE. *Theatre in a Tent: The Development of a Provincial Entertainment.* Bowling Green, O.: Bowling Green Univ. Popular Press, 1972. Compares RT's Jonathan to the red-mopped Toby character of the tent shows. Valid. See esp. pp. 86 - 88.

SPENGEMANN, WILLIAM C. *The Adventurous Muse: The Poetics of American Fiction, 1789 - 1900.* New Haven: Yale University Press, 1977. Chapter Three is entitled "The Adventurous Muse: 'The Algerine Captive' and 'Arthur Gordon Pym.' " Spengemann considers *Captive* to be "the first American novel to break through the formal and ideological restrictions imposed upon stories of travel by domestic tradition. . ." (p. 119).

TANSELLE, G. THOMAS. *Royall Tyler.* Cambridge, Mass.: Harvard Univ. Press, 1967. Outstanding scholarship; the first published full-length critical biography of RT.

TOWER, NOREEN. "A Critical Study of Royall Tyler's *The Contrast*." M.A. thesis, Univ. of Oklahoma, 1961. A few errors; some perceptive comments.

TYLER, MARY PALMER. *Grandmother Tyler's Book*. Ed. Frederick Tupper and Helen Tyler Brown. New York: G. P. Putnam's, 1925. Essential for RT scholars. Fascinating reading. Includes memoirs of Elizabeth Hunt Palmer. The MSS of both memoirs are at the VHS.

———. *The Maternal Physician: A Treatise on the Nurture and Management of Infants From the Birth Until Two Years Old. Being the Result of Sixteen Years' Experience in the Nursery*. New York: Isaac Riley, 1811; 2nd ed. Philadelphia: Lewis Adams, 1818. Interesting, sensible, occasionally (and unconsciously) humorous. Valuable source of information for students of early nineteenth-century family life in America.

"TYLER, ROYALL." *National Cyclopaedia of American Biography*. New York: James T. White, 1897. Short but adequate biography. See Vol. VII, p. 39.

TYLER, THOMAS PICKMAN. "Memoir of Royall Tyler." Unpubl. MS in VHS. Essential source of information for serious students of RT. Contains many anecdotes about RT's life, biographical information, letters, etc. Also see A. L. Carson and H. L. Carson, "Outline for TPT's *Memoir of Royall Tyler*," unpubl. MS, VHS.

Index

DATE DUE
